LAUGHING AND CRYING ALONE

LES LUCK
Laughing and Crying Alone

Charleston, SC
www.PalmettoPublishing.com

Laughing and Crying Alone

Copyright © 2023 by Les Luck

Front Cover image by Salvacion Tejada

All rights reserved

No portion of this book may be reproduced, stored in a retrieval system, or transmitted in any form by any means–electronic, mechanical, photocopy, recording, or other–except for brief quotations in printed reviews, without prior permission of the author.

First Edition

Paperback ISBN: 979-8-8229-1328-8

eBook ISBN: 979-8-8229-1329-5

*I dedicate this book to my "mum."
I will love you always.
You told me to reach for the sky, and I did.*

Ding Dong Ditch and Crawdads

Lisa Villalobos was eleven years old. She loved her cousins like they were her brothers. They went on little adventures through their neighborhood, riding their bikes everywhere. They did dumb things that kids sometimes do.

They went door to door, ringing the doorbells and then running as fast as they could away from the neighbors' places. They never got caught. <u>Sometimes</u> they throw stink bombs on the porches so the neighbors would find a nice surprise when they answered the door.

They also went door to door, collecting old newspapers. They had no use for them whatsoever. They just thought it would be fun to collect piles of the stuff. They wanted a friendly connection with the people but also just really didn't have anything better to do.

The boys and Lisa would walk down to the creek and catch crawdads. They had no desire to eat them but watched their uncle cook them anyway. Lisa loved their little adventures. She was a kid with no cares in the world.

Cousin Iris and the Official Bear Club

Iris was Lisa's cousin. She was so adorable with long, curly hair, and glasses. They started The Official Bear Club with T-shirts and all. They loved teddy bears so much and they even wrote a theme song. Lisa loved her cousin so much. They went to hip-hop concerts at the local amusement park and flirted with boys from fourteen years old. They would spend several days at each other's house in the summertime. Lisa was boy-crazy, and Iris knew it. She helped her meet a boy at Iris's friend's house, but they had to be sneaky about it. Hanging out with boys was a no no. One day when Lisa was twelve years old, she wore so much makeup and fixed her hair like a grownup. Her aunt found her and looked so shocked to see her niece with tons of makeup on her pretty, young face. Lisa hoped her aunt didn't notice that she had stuffed her bra as well. Lisa couldn't stop thinking about boys. Their Official Bear Club became a thing of the past, and all Lisa wanted to do was meet boys secretly. Iris kept her secrets safe, though, because she loved Lisa so much.

Mason

Lisa was now fourteen years old and in the ninth grade. She thought she was in love. Mason was so handsome, and they would talk on the phone for several minutes, sometimes an hour. He was a Black guy; his skin was a honey color, and his brown eyes complemented his fuzzy, short, brown hair. She could feel her heart beat faster every time he was in her presence. The so-called relationship went on for a few weeks, but they never kissed. They would hold hands, or he would put his arm around her, but that was about it. One day he told her that he was in love with a gal named Martha. She was so beautiful. Her hazel eyes glistened in the sun along with her wavy, long, brown hair. She was a tiny little thing with large breasts. Mason told her he liked Martha instead and that she was a *hot product*. He broke Lisa's heart. She went home in tears.

Her mother comforted her. She gave her one long hug and said there would be many more guys that would be after her, much more handsome than that turkey, Mason. Lisa tried to let go of him; she really did. While she sat at her desk in home room one day, Mason grabbed her breast quickly and smiled at her. He thought she would be pleased by this. She stormed out of the room. She couldn't stop thinking about the incident and went home very stressed. The incident triggered a nerve. She stopped eating and drinking, then started seeing things and hearing voices.

Voices

Lisa didn't eat. She used to love the school's nachos, but seeing any type of food made her want to throw up. She couldn't focus on school, and then she started to lose sleep. She started going through the motions of everyday school life but couldn't quite find her *normal* self. She was an empty shell. The hallucinations started. In math class, she would read word problems that wouldn't make any sense. In one word problem, she read that Susan had eleven assholes instead of apples. It didn't trouble her at first until she started to hear the voices.

She didn't know what the voices were saying. They sounded robotic and loud, and they wouldn't stop. It scared the hell out of her. Her father drove her home from school, and they would pound in her head for minutes at a time. She pretended not to hear them, but really, she was so scared. Her mother and father started to worry, especially when she told her mother to kill her.

"Mom, please kill me. I am a bad person. Please just kill me!" she cried and was confused.

Her mother told her she did nothing wrong, and she begged her to eat. "Eat, baby. What is wrong? Why won't you eat?" She bought her all her favorite fast food like Taco Bell or Kentucky Fried Chicken, but Lisa took one look at the food and had no desire to eat anything. She felt like a frozen body, cold and with no emotions.

At home she started acting like a stereotypical Black person; she looked at her father and said, "I can't sing no mo'! I can't sing no mo'!"

He didn't understand why she was saying this, but she was trying to express that things weren't as they should be. She really couldn't sing though. She tried, but her voice just wouldn't come out. For God's sake, she was hearing voices and seeing weird words in books that weren't there. She wanted to feel normal again. She wanted the voices to go away, and she wanted to eat again.

The First Hospital

Lisa's mother took her to a child psychiatrist who prescribed medications for her anxiety and psychosis. One of these medications made her bladder shut down, and she had to wear a damn catheter. That thing was so painful. Imagine being pierced by a tiny tube down there. She hated it. She had to walk around with a bag attached to her leg. Her parents had to deal with this, and she felt like this big baby who couldn't do anything. The medications made the psychoses worse, and her mother and father decided she should be admitted into a psychiatric hospital.

They took her shoelaces as a safety precaution. She had to wear rubber bands around her shoes to keep them on. She felt like a fool. Immediately, she wanted to go home. Lisa was assigned a roommate and she seemed pretty nice. She was an overweight Latina girl, always smiling. Lisa never knew why the girl was there exactly; she seemed perfectly fine to her. Lisa even gave her a special gold bracelet for being her special friend. Her mother asked the girl to give Lisa back the bracelet, but she wouldn't.

Then there was Seth. He was a skinny, redheaded boy with braces, and Lisa immediately liked him. He was definitely depressed, but she could tell that he was trying hard to get better. Every morning he would knock on Lisa's door. "Lisa, it's time for our exercises." She would go sometimes, but most days, she wanted to just lie in bed like a blob of nothingness. She felt no desire to do anything. She didn't want to go to the group meetings and activities. She was always forced into participating.

One of the mental health workers yelled at her in the dining room to eat. "You are not leaving until you eat something!" She started to stand up and the mental health worker pushed her down. "Eat."

That happened on most days. The food tasted like shit. When she was "normal, "she loved all food; she would eat almost anything. But this food tasted like death. The juice was too cold for her mouth, and sometimes when she drank, she could feel juice dribble out of her mouth as though she had just been to the dentist. Potatoes tasted like nothing, and the mushy texture bothered her mouth.

One day Lisa decided she wanted to die. She had had enough of everything. She was tired of seeing roommates come and go. She was tired of this hospital and tired of the world. She swallowed the entire contents of the sam-

The First Hospital

ple-sized bottle of shampoo from her room. She thought to herself that surely she would die if she swallowed all that shampoo. She started to gag and went into the hallway. This was a cry for help and attention. Why was she dumb enough to think that would even kill her? She was a dumb suicidal all right. She thought to herself how nice it would be to die. The hospital workers pinned her down and had her drink tons of water. Then when they knew she was fine, they sent her to the quiet room.

The quiet room was exactly what it was. It was a room with a bed with white sheets, and that was it. Because she felt freer in the quiet room, she would do things just to get sent there. She even tried to escape the stupid hospital by throwing her body against emergency exit doors. The hospital workers pinned her down and put her in the quiet room again. Just what she wanted.

One day in the quiet room, she had her worst panic attack ever. Thank God her mother was there with her. "Breathe Lisa. Take a deep breath. Don't forget to breathe." Lisa would run out of breath, and her chest felt like it was falling deep into a pit. She felt like she was going to die, and nobody around made it any better—not the doctors, the hospital workers, the priest, not a damn person. Eventually, the panic attack stopped.

Lisa cried in the quiet room a lot, but it wasn't a full-on cry. She felt like she had lost her voice. She had loved to sing. One of the hospital workers comforted her and sang to her; Lisa cried even more and tried to sing along with her. When the worker left, she tried so hard to sing, but only a few words came out. "Lean on me. Lean on me." She couldn't sing even though she tried so hard. She wanted to yell, but she just couldn't do it. She felt like she was trapped in her own body, which used to be able to do human things.

One day Lisa was able to go on an outing with her father, her aunt, and her aunt's husband. They took her to KFC because they knew she loved it. She acted pretty normal and had a great time. They hoped that she would be coming home soon. That night she went to her hospital room and put the leftover fries on her dresser. Damn it, she thought to herself. The French fries had smiley faces on them, and they started to shake. She started to eat them, and they shook as she ate them. She was so damn frustrated.

One day in the quiet room, Lisa was napping but woke up from her nap and hallucinated an odd picture. She stared at the wooden door, and within the door's wavy, wooden lines, she saw Jesus Christ wearing DJ headphones, spinning records on a turntable. She loved this hallucination; it was like he was telling her to wake up and that everything would be OK. So Lisa started trying to get better. She woke up and started to think of all the people she loved and who loved her back. She started to think of volleyball and choir. Her friend Martha even

The First Hospital

came to visit her and brought her a nice plant to put in her room. Lisa resented her just a little since Mason was in love with her, but Lisa appreciated her presence.

She started to take her medications. Before, she would pretend to swallow them but managed to hide the medication under her tongue; she would spit them out and give them to her hospital buddy-friend Lee. He wanted them for whatever reason. But now she complied with the nurses and swallowed the medication. She started listening to her Walkman again, but then it was stolen. This was her second Walkman; the first one had also been stolen, and her mother refused to buy her a third. But still, she heard her favorite songs in her head by choice. She started writing in her journal. She wrote rhymes, positive ones to take with her after the hospital stay. She started to eat. Finally the food tasted good. She could actually smell the mashed potatoes, and instead of feeling like cold, useless mush, they sort of burnt her tongue and actually tasted like potatoes. The juice tasted like juice, and it wasn't too cold this time. After all of this, she started to get better, and she was able to go home.

Lisa got home but was still a little off. Her friends noticed she really wasn't herself. She hid in one of the restroom stalls and her friend Clarisa said, "Lisa, are you OK?" Lisa laughed nervously; she wanted to tell her that she wasn't OK, but she said nothing.

It took a few months to get back to feeling centered after her mother had her psychiatrist stop all the meds. This was an abrupt transition for her, but she made it through. With sleep and supportive family and friends, she got through it.

Fifteen Years Later

Lisa had just given birth to a beautiful baby girl, but her heart felt heavy; she wanted to talk to her mother, Sundee Santis, but she and her mother weren't speaking. Lisa was hoping her mother would visit, but Sundee had been too hurt to come to see her. They had exchanged harsh words months before she delivered baby Zoey. This was Sundee's third grandchild, and Lisa wanted her to be there to help her get through it, as a mother should. Zoey was asleep, so she decided to phone Sundee from the hospital.

"Hello," Sundee said. She sounded a bit annoyed but still curious.

"Hey, Mom. I just had the baby."

"Yeah, I know. Your sisters told me."

Lisa, at that moment, thought her mother sounded so cold. She wanted to ask her why she didn't come visit her granddaughter.

"Well, I just wanted to hear your voice, that's all!" Lisa said, with her voice trembling.

She hung up after being so brash. She was hurting, and she wept in her hospital bed. She felt pathetic, like a sick child. Lisa needed Sundee. She needed her to run her hands through her tangled hair. Lisa still loved her and needed her presence.

Three Months Later

Lisa couldn't sleep. The baby wasn't exactly sleeping through the night, so she sure was awake a lot. Lisa would change her diapers and nurse her to sleep. It was a simple cycle. She felt so needed and excited to have a third child, but also very exhausted. She stayed up late at night, happy to be needed. She was enthralled with being an infant's mother again. She loved knowing her baby needed her.

Lisa started thinking of Sundee again. She remembered her childhood and how close they had been. She would embrace her a lot, kiss her cheeks, and smell her newly washed hair. She made her laugh. Lisa needed her to be a part of her life again.

Zoey was three months old, and Sundee still hadn't met her. Lisa remembered when her mother had helped her through labor with her first child, Justin. Sundee had gently rubbed her back and braided Lisa's hair, so it would be out of her face. She had felt so safe having Sundee there with her. Her mother-in-law had been there too, but having her own mother there was special.

Lisa started to weep again. She missed her mother so much. She decided to call her, but she wasn't sure about what she would say exactly.

"Mom?" Her voice was trembling.

"Yeah?"

"I miss you so much. I'm sorry it's been so long, but I really miss you."

They didn't talk for very long but decided they would see each other soon.

Before seeing her mother, she was contemplating using birth control pills. What she should've done was have a tubal ligation while she was in the hospital, having Zoey, her third and final child. Her husband, Zachariah, was against it because he was a bit scared of the procedure. He kept telling her that he would get a vasectomy soon. Still, Lisa did not want to get pregnant ever again. Zoey made their little family complete—Lisa, Zachariah, Justin, Joey, and Zoey. Their special little family. They would always stick together.

Lisa had never heard of this particular brand of birth control before, but they made her feel weird. She wasn't quite herself. She was always anxious and felt super emotional. She left a message for her doctor; she wanted to make sure it would be OK to take them since she was breastfeeding. He asked her if she wanted to take a different pill. She told him if he thought this was all right while nursing, she would go on with it. He told her to monitor herself and make sure she was producing enough milk for the baby.

Lisa went to the pharmacy to pick up her prescription. She requested the generic medication as it would save her a little money. They asked her if she had ever taken this medication and if she would like to talk with the pharmacist. She agreed. The pharmacist was a very stern-looking Asian woman, Chinese. Her hair was straight and short, cut just a little below her ears. She wore glasses and an official-looking white coat. She explained how to use the pills droning on and on.

Lisa asked her, "Are the side effects of this generic brand the same as the name brand?" The bitch's nostrils flared, and she pursed her lips.

"The side effects are the SAME!"

Lisa was shocked at how rude she was. She didn't bother thanking her. She crumpled the paper bag with the pills in it and walked away, very frustrated and very concerned. Lisa's mother-in-law and sister-in-law kept telling her it would be fine.

A Daughter's Visit

A few days later, Lisa started taking the birth control pills. She decided to surprise Sundee with a visit from her and her three kids. Her oldest son, Justin, was almost seven years old, and her second child, Joey, had just turned three. Zoey was three months old. Lisa was feeling very emotional. She hadn't slept very well, but her body felt OK. She was energetic, actually. Her allergies were bothering her, but for some reason, the pseudoephedrine made her feel better all around. She was feeling like she was on top of the world. She would see her mother, and Sundee would finally meet the granddaughter she'd always hoped for. Lisa and her eighteen-year-old sister, Coco, kept texting each other. Coco was with Sundee, running errands. After Lisa bought her favorite dark-chocolate-chip truffles at See's Candies, Coco filled Lisa in on their next stop. Lisa would see Sundee at Starbucks. Lisa was driving toward Starbucks very excited. She really needed her mother in her life. She walked into Starbucks with the

A Daughter's Visit

double stroller. Sundee's back was turned; she was drinking coffee and talking to Coco. Coco gestured for Sundee to turn around and she did. Lisa started to cry. Lisa was so happy to see Sundee's beautiful face. She hadn't seen her in several months. Zoey was sitting innocently in her stroller, kicking her legs and drooling. She wore a purple one-piece, pajama-like outfit. Purple was Sundee's favorite color. She looked at her granddaughter and smiled so big.

"She looks like you," she said to Lisa.

Tears filled Lisa's eyes and dripped quickly down her face. She could feel people staring, but she didn't care. Sundee tried hard not to cry, but Lisa could feel her relief at seeing them. She was sure Sundee missed her and wanted to see her new grandchild. She was ecstatic.

Paranoia

Lisa's husband, Zachariah Case, was taking antidepressants because he was having a lot of trouble at work. He had been given more to do, difficult tasks he thought he couldn't handle. He felt so much pressure. He knew he had to take care of his family, and having a third child added to his stress; he felt inadequate, as if he was failing them. The truth was that he was a walking zombie because of the medication. He thought he needed the medication, so he continued with the pills, but he was so distant and so numb.

In the evening, he told Lisa that he had run out of medicine and that he needed her to get a refill for him. Lisa agreed to go to the pharmacy, and he was relieved. She even agreed to take Justin and Zoey. At the pharmacy, Lisa felt super alert. She felt like everything around her was a blur as she honed in on her son Justin. He was organizing products on a shelf, turning them to look nice and symmetrical. He looked at her and gave her an innocent smile. He sat back down with her and said he wasn't feeling well.

"When we get home, you want me to make you some warm Ovaltine?" she asked.

He nodded and smiled. He noticed a man from the cleaning staff. "Mommy, that man is looking at you," he said.

She told him not to worry about it. She picked up her husband's prescription, and they walked out of the pharmacy. The man smiled at Lisa and looked at Zoey. He asked how old she was, and Lisa smiled and told him she was three months old. He said he had a granddaughter that was born on a particular day. Not even thinking about it, she said, "That's a good number." He gave her a puzzled look, and she walked out of the building with her children and into the parking lot. It was the weirdest thing, as it wasn't what Lisa said but how she said it. The man was probably turned off by her bubbly attitude. Perhaps she came on too strong, overly friendly, and comfortable with him, a complete stranger.

Lisa felt so high, like she could accomplish so much. She felt ambitious and was looking forward to going home to be a mommy again to the baby. She put the boys to bed and then Zoey and Lisa hung out in the living room. Lisa watched television, a lot of it. It was getting late, but still, she watched it like an addict. She didn't even pay attention to the program; she was enjoying the euphoric feeling. She was alive, and she was a mother to a beautiful infant who needed Lisa, who would stay up and pull an all-nighter. She has pulled all-nighters before. She used to stay up all night, studying for tests in college. As a mother, she used to pull all-nighters to clean her kitchen.

Zachariah came out of the bedroom around one in the morning. "You need to go to sleep, honey. Remember, you're a mom."

The nerve of him. She thought that was a silly thing to say, and it made her want to stay up even later. She didn't even know if she slept. She got up at six, ready to take Justin to first grade. Sundee had called for some reason, and Lisa told her that Justin wasn't feeling well. Sundee convinced her that he was probably faking and to take him to school anyway. Lisa listened to her mother and didn't even bother taking Justin's temperature. By the time she got everybody ready, they were running late. Lisa felt so nervous. He was going to be thirty minutes late to class. Lisa was so embarrassed and scared at the same time.

For some reason, Lisa was paranoid to leave the apartment. Then she realized that she was afraid that somebody was going to take her children away, just snatch one of them. Now that there were three of them, she had to be extremely careful and put her guard up against the evil, harsh world. They got to the school office, and she noticed a quiet sensation and felt that everyone in that office was watching her every move. She felt paranoid. She asked the lady in the front office for a tardy slip; the lady wrote one up and looked at her smiling.

"You've got your hands full," she said.

Lisa smiled and sighed a bit of relief. She walked Justin to his classroom. They entered the classroom without knocking. Lisa saw all the children look at her, and only her. She felt all their little eyes on her, and it creeped her out. She felt like they were watching her every move. The teacher was going about her own business. Lisa apologized as they walked in, and the teacher said it was all right. Justin acted like he wanted to be away from his mother, so school was a blessing for him at that particular moment. He knew something was off about Lisa. He needed her to be in her right mind, and she wasn't acting like her normal self. Something was wrong, but she couldn't cry out for help. She just didn't have it in her to tell anyone what she was feeling. Lisa thought *they* would take her kids away if they didn't go to school. She was extremely paranoid.

Panic Attack

Lisa had been on the pill for two days and really felt off. Her allergies were bugging her too, so she took the pseudoephedrine again, remembering how much better it would make her feel. That night she couldn't sleep again. She needed someone's support. It was 2:00 a.m., so she called her twenty-year-old sister, who was always up late. Shannen happened to be in the area, and she asked Lisa if she wanted her to come over. She agreed. They ate Filipino food that their aunt had made; it tasted so good. Lisa and her sister talked about nonsensical things, and after they ate, they went into the living room.

"Shannen, can you massage my feet?" Lisa asked.

"If you really want me to, I will," she replied.

Lisa asked her why she would do that for her.

"Because I love you," she said.

After Shannen massaged her feet, Lisa hugged her goodbye. Lisa felt so much better after her visit. The next morning she woke up at six, after about two hours of sleep.

Justin had a fever this time, so she called the school's sick line and felt so horrible. She had sent him to school the previous day sick.

The day went on as normal, but that evening Lisa experienced her second major panic attack. While talking on the phone with her sister Shannen, Lisa told her that she was feeling stressed and felt something weird coming on. She hung up quickly and felt her chest drop.

"Ahhhh!" she screamed. "Zach! I can't breathe. I can't breathe. Help me!"

Justin started to freak out. He was so vulnerable to stressful situations; he knew his father wasn't invincible after he had come home with a very bruised head and eye one day in the past. Zach had gotten into a fight with a few men at a bar on a work night. Lisa was pregnant at the time and begged him to come home but he wouldn't. Her son was insecure about his father, and seeing his mother fall apart was rocking his world.

Justin started to cry and shout, "Is Mommy going to die?"

Lisa bawled irrationally and couldn't help acting like she was indeed going to die. She bawled and screamed. She ran to her bedroom and buried her head into a pillow. Zach prompted her to just breathe.

"You're having a panic attack. You're not going to die," he said.

Her knees were shaking, and she could feel her whole body sweat. They called the hospital's advice line, and they instructed Lisa to do some breathing exercises. The symptoms stopped, and they told her to stop taking that God-awful pill. Her mother-in-law, Ore-Ida Rachel, took her to the ER, and Lisa felt better then. Lisa's mobile phone was running out of minutes—she had a pay-as-you-go plan. She accidentally put one hundred dollars on the account. After the transaction went through, she realized what she had done and decided to call customer service to get the matter resolved. It was serious as she and Zach didn't have the money in the bank. They were already trying to get on top of their finances and all the insufficient-fund fees.

Ore-Ida waited in the ER lobby, and Lisa told her she would be right back. She went into the restroom and called the mobile phone company, getting through to customer service. As she was put on hold, she heard a techno sort of sound. It really was a mellow-sounding tune. But to Lisa, that night it was very electric, techno sounding, and it captured her, mesmerized her in a very weird way. She was in a trance. A while later, someone from customer service came on and said they would help her resolve the situation.

They kept putting Lisa on hold until she finally said, "Listen, I'm in the middle of a major panic attack, and I need this transaction reversed, so you've got to help me."

After everything was done, she called her grad-school friend Fran.

Fran told her that exercise was the best thing to remedy anxiety. Lisa thanked her for the advice and then ran around one wing of the hospital. A young security guard followed Lisa, looking at her as though she had two heads.

"Hi, I am just trying to run to get rid of some anxiety I was feeling," she explained.

He smiled, and she asked him if he went to school, and he said he went to a nearby community college. Lisa asked if he was going to take a public speaking class since she used to teach it, and he said he was. She told him that she taught at the local public university, and he seemed somewhat interested. She waved goodbye to him and went back into the ER lobby.

Her mother-in-law looked at her and said with relief, "I was wondering where you went."

After Lisa told her about the mobile phone situation, she heard her name called out by one of the nurses.

The nurse was gorgeous. She had a pretty face, and her long, silky hair came down to her bottom. She looked Hawaiian. As she took Lisa's blood pressure, she asked her what was going on. Lisa told her she just had a major panic attack, and the nurse asked Lisa if it felt like impending doom. Lisa told her it did, and the nurse sent her to the next station to take care of her co-pay, which was fifty dollars. She didn't have this, so her mother-in-law, Ore-Ida, helped her pay even though she was hurting financially too. Lisa went into the doctor's office and told him her story.

Lisa didn't let the doctor get a word in edgewise. He was trying to explain to her something about her hormones, and she cut him off. He could hear that Lisa's speech was slurred and that she wasn't making any sense. He told her she had a colorful personality and that he would give her valium to calm her down. She immediately froze.

"I'm nursing right now. Will this be OK for the baby?" she asked.

After a little research, he told her he wasn't sure if it would hurt the baby. What the hell, she thought to herself. She started to tell him she was ready to stop nursing, but he cut her off this time and told her she was to make a follow-up appointment with her doctor and prescribed her exercise in the meantime. Lisa wanted to scream. She needed help fast, but nobody seemed to care.

Lisa's Date with Mom

Lisa's mother heard about her anxiety and wanted to pick her up. She told her to take a shower first.

"You're coming with me. We're going to lunch," she said.

They arrived at the restaurant and were trying to park the car, but two guys were in the way. They started to walk out of the way.

"Excuse me, gentleman," Lisa said in a flirtatious tone. In her right mind, she would have just kept her mouth shut, but she was compelled to be noticed. They just smiled.

Sundee took Lisa to a Thai restaurant, the one Lisa's father and she used to go to.

"Mom, some day I would like for you, my dad, and me to have lunch, just us three," she said. Lisa's parents were divorced and civil, but Lisa's mother still had issues with seeing him in person. She agreed to make Lisa happy at the time.

Sundee made Lisa laugh in the restaurant. She laughed so hard that people stared. Sundee put her finger to her mouth. "Shhh!" Sundee said. Lisa immediately stopped laughing. She realized she was definitely being loud, too loud for a public restaurant for that matter. They left the restaurant and went to Lisa's hairdresser, but they didn't have an appointment.

"Hi, Lynn! Can I get a haircut?"

Lynn looked at her like she was from outer space and said, "We're busy, Lisa!"

"OK, Lynn, we'll go somewhere else," Lisa said.

Lynn waved but still seemed a bit concerned since Lisa was not acting like herself, for sure. Lisa could see by the expression on Lynn's face that she was worried about her. Her mother then took her to her own hairdresser, and Lisa got a cute bob and a manicure.

As Lisa was getting her nails done, she noticed her mother acting nervous. Sundee kept staring at her, and every time Lisa started to open her mouth to talk to the manicurist, Sundee shook her head and pursed her lips as if to tell her to keep her mouth shut. Lisa was acting strangely, and Sundee needed her to stop. They finished the mini makeover and got in the car. Lisa could feel the anxiety in her chest and held her breath. They went to the store to buy some antacids for Lisa's supposed heartburn, but Lisa was really having pre–panic attack episodes. They bought some Coronas, too, to help her relax. By this time, Lisa needed to go home to nurse the baby.

Spa Fran

Lisa called Fran, one of her good college friends, and told her she was having major anxiety and that everyone said she wasn't acting like herself. She needed a break from everyone. Fran told Lisa to come to *Spa Fran*. Lisa first leaves her place then takes a shower at Fran's. Lisa left her home in her pajamas, taking a change of clothes. After the shower, Lisa started to relax. She became a little compulsive, though, because she stared at her face in the mirror for several minutes and decided she needed to tweeze her eyebrows. She couldn't handle the way they looked anymore. Borrowing tweezers from Fran, Lisa tweezed her eyebrows, looked in the mirror, and smiled. It was a bit eerie what she saw. It was like she was looking at a different reflection, someone with clear skin, and someone who was as confident as ever.

After a tour of Fran's house, they went into the dining room, where she had burritos and pizza rolls ready for them.

"How did you know these are my favorites?" Lisa asked.

Fran just smiled and handed her a burrito. Lisa ate it quickly, but Fran could tell she didn't want the whole thing. Lisa was forcing herself to eat it, but Fran said, "Lisa, just toss it! It's OK!"

So Lisa tossed the burrito, and they went into the living room. By this time, Zach had called Fran to tell her to bring Lisa home because the baby was hungry. Fran said they'd stay for just twenty more minutes. They talked about friends, and Lisa started imitating some of them. She thought she was being hysterical, but she wasn't making any sense. Fran was very understanding.

On the drive home, Lisa's speech was slurred. They talked about their graduate theses, and Lisa kept saying *thingy* to replace words she didn't know. She must have said *thingy* a thousand times. She told Fran to stop driving so terribly and then apologized. They arrived at Lisa's place, and Fran met Zach at the entryway of their apartment complex. She whispered something into his ear and hugged him. She told him to take good care of Lisa.

Earlier, before they had left for Fran's, Fran had reassured the family that Lisa wasn't a danger to herself. After Lisa got home, they called the doctor's office and were told he'd call right back. Lisa was soon on the phone with one of the psychiatrists.

He started explaining and said, "When a woman has just had a baby, her hormones—" But she cut him off.

"Listen, pal, don't tell me anything. This isn't the way you talk to someone with a panic disorder. Have you ever given birth?" she asked coldly.

"Yes, with my wife," he answered.

She hung up the phone, and her husband was so confused.

"What did he say?" Zach asked.

She told him not to worry. A woman called back and said the previous doctor was sorry for his behavior. She told Lisa to make sure she went to see her doctor soon.

On a High

Lisa was feeling restless.

"Get some sleep. We'll go to the doctor in the morning," her husband said.

She had an appointment the next day with the doctor as she was feeling off again. She lay in bed, worried. She was scared because she didn't know what was happening to her. She closed her eyes but found herself getting out of bed every five minutes to check on her daughter. She was afraid Zoey would die of SIDS (sudden infant death syndrome) like her dear friend's daughter did years ago. She slept for a little while. She woke up at 4:00 a.m. feeling a sudden rush of energy.

Lisa felt like she'd slept for a good few hours but later realized she must have slept for one hour. It had been four nights since she'd gotten a good night's rest, maybe five. She got up and decided to get her mini radio, put her earphones on, and work out in the kitchen. She started to feel spiritual, as if God was sending messages to her through different forms of media. She heard songs on the radio that she thought God was making her hear. "I feel the earth move under my feet!" she sang along, and boy, did she really feel the earth move under her feet. She felt on top of the world. Then she heard the song "Jump Around" by House of Pain and she lost control. She danced hard and yelled out, "Go, Lisa! It's your birthday! Go, Lisa! It's your birthday!" Zach woke up and asked if she was OK. She told him she was working out. "Is that a crime?" she asked.

Lisa wanted to bump her volleyball around but found it flat. She looked for the pump and couldn't find it, so she decided to watch TV. "OK, God, what are you trying to tell me?" she asked. She turned the TV on, and her favorite movie of all time was playing. *See No Evil, Hear No Evil* was at her favorite part where Richard Pryor sticks an ice cream cone in Gene Wilder's hair. She thought God was truly playing a joke on her. What's next, God? What is next?

Zachariah decided to call in sick and stay with Lisa as she was acting a fool the whole morning. She was neighing like a horse every so often and running around the house saying, "Don't hate me because I'm beautiful!" She was laughing at absolutely nothing, and she woke up the neighbors with her loud, obnoxious laugh. Zach was crying, burying his head in his hands. Lisa walked over to him and asked him if he needed a hug. He gestured for her to go away.

"Wiggity wiggity wiggity wiggity whack mama, wiggity wiggity wiggity wiggity whack!" Lisa shouted. She paced back and forth. Zach called the doctor and set up an appointment for two days later. Lisa calmed down after a while, and Zach didn't know what to do.

A few hours later, Zach urged his wife to get some sleep. She drummed on her son's bedroom dresser. "Bump chooka chooka, bump chooka chooka," she sang. Her son drummed along with her, but he looked so scared. She went to the bathroom and sang songs as loud as she could. She also brushed her teeth so harshly that her gums bled. She could be heard blocks away, but they let her sing anyway. Her mother and aunt made lumpia and okoy, Filipino food they thought would comfort her. Lisa's sister Coco and cousin Liz came to visit and to see the state Lisa was in. She ate, and still, she acted a fool. Her mother mentioned that Lisa was giving a performance and that they had free tickets to the show. She was imitating family members and pacing back and forth. She did some of the dishes but didn't finish them.

Negative Energy

Later on after everyone left, Lisa calmed down for a bit. She watched *Ellen*, putting the TV on full blast while her boys were trying to get some sleep. She ate pizza and drank a whole jug of apple juice, which she would never do in her right mind. It was a school night. She just wanted to be herself. It felt so good to be herself, she thought. She wasn't making any sense. Zach begged her to get some sleep, so she tried hard and managed to get a little bit but woke up in the middle of the night.

Lisa took all the framed pictures off the walls as she felt they had negative energy. She took certain Christmas cards off the wall and told Zach that these cards were giving her messages. One of the cards had a picture of a father holding his baby girl in his lap, with the caption, "A King is Born." She thought the picture was trying to say this girl would grow up to be transgendered or gay because of the word *king*. Zach started to freak out. He was trying to hide his panic, but it showed. Lisa took a shower as he cried in the living room. After the shower she called her mother-in-law. "Ore-Ida Rachel Case, get your ass over here right now, you drama queen. Your son is flipping out. He is going crazy," she said.

Lisa told him to close the curtains as he was smoking out on the patio. She had just gotten out of the shower and was wearing a towel. She felt someone was watching, someone outside. After arguing back and forth, she slapped Zach, and he threatened to call the police. She told him to go right ahead because he was the one who needed to be locked up. This time Zach took her to the ER.

"What's wrong, Lisa? Where's my Lisa? Where did she go?" he asked.

"This is me," she said.

She started to cry as she felt his words hurt a little. Minutes later she started to put on a façade, pretending everything was OK. She fooled the nurse, or at least she thought she did. She and Zach had decided to bring the baby, and she could sense Zach's fear. She wanted to act as calmly as she could, hoping the nurse would think he was the crazy one. After she took her blood pressure, Zach told the ER nurse that Lisa had an appointment the next day. She told them to make sure Lisa made that appointment. They left the ER and returned home. Zachariah begged Lisa to sleep again, but she just couldn't, no matter how hard she tried.

51/50

The next morning, even though Zach knew that Lisa had an appointment at 2 p.m., he decided he would take her in at 10 a.m.

"Why are we going so early?" she asked.

"We're going to see if they can take you early, that's all," he said. She couldn't find her purse which had her ID in it. "Don't worry. You're my wife. They'll help us," he said. Their two sons were hugging each other right before they left. She kissed them and the baby goodbye. For some reason, she knew she wasn't coming home that day.

On the drive from home, Lisa thought she had a special ability to see the past. She thought she could see into Zach's past. She felt so sorry for him because she thought she could feel his pain. They parked the car and tried to check in early. They were given some paperwork to fill out so they went back to the car to do so. She felt his childhood pain again. She thought she had a special ability to feel this pain. He had had three important people in his life die when he was a young age, and she thought she could feel the pain from all of that. After he was done filling out the paperwork, Zach took her to the sidewalk so he could smoke a cigarette. She felt so cold. She felt that everything was so cold. She felt like she was going to be on a TV show, waiting for cameras to appear. She didn't see any cameras. Lisa heard dogs barking in a van, and they were so loud.

"Zach, they're trying to tell me something," she said.

"Honey, they're fine. They're just barking," he said.

"No, look, they're really trying to tell me something!" she yelled.

He ignored her. She saw an elderly woman all by herself, waiting for someone to pick her up.

"Do you need help?" Lisa asked her.

"No, I'm fine. I'm waiting for my granddaughter to pick me up."

Immediately after she said that, like magic, the granddaughter appeared. She smiled at Lisa nervously. Lisa smiled back, and she could feel Zach tense up at that moment. He was so embarrassed.

They went into the lobby of the psychiatry department. After he handed the paperwork to the lady at the front desk, Zach begged the lady to squeeze them in as the appointment was urgent. He had no clue what was going on with Lisa and thought he had lost her forever to some sort of craziness. They waited in the lobby for a few minutes and then heard Lisa's name called. They were put in a meeting room, where they waited for the psychiatrist to show up. Zach left her to go to the restroom. She got up on top of a table and started to write on the whiteboard.

Lisa crossed out words on the board that she thought didn't make any sense and replaced them with words she thought made sense. Zach came in.

"Lisa, why are you on the table? Please, get down from there. You might get hurt," he said.

She came down, but by this time, a security guard had entered the room and started to observe her. She passed gas several times, and loudly.

"I'm sorry, is it OK if I fart?" she asked.

The security guard said it was OK with him, and Zach laughed nervously. She felt a little guilty for passing gas in the meeting room, so she went to the restroom. She thought she was on a reality show, *Candid Camera* perhaps. On her way to the restroom, she went through the lobby.

"I have to go to the restroom so I can fart," she said to the two elderly ladies in the lobby, who laughed.

She thought she was hilarious. Where are the cameras, she thought to herself. After she came out of the restroom, Zach and the security guard followed her back into the meeting room.

By this time Lisa wanted to play a game. She thought she could feel people's presence and feel their energy, dead or alive. She asked the security guard what his full name was, and he told her. She wrote it down on the whiteboard and associated his name somehow with his grandmother, and she told him she was sending him positive energy. Then she did this with Zachariah; he was so frustrated and scared for her at the same time. He thought he had lost her for good.

A therapist came in to talk with Lisa, and Lisa thought she could feel the woman's negative energy. The therapist looked at her while Lisa explained that Zach wasn't listening to her. She had short hair and a pretty face, and for some reason, while Lisa looked at her hair, she could feel the therapist looking at her in a way that was judgmental. Lisa told her brashly to go away because of her negative energy. A psychiatrist came in a few minutes later and told Lisa she was going to the hospital.

"I don't want to," she said.

"Sorry, but you have to," she replied.

"I like your necklace," Lisa said out of the blue. The psychiatrist had on a piece made strictly of buttons; blue ones, gray ones, purple ones, and other colors.

"Thank you. I am glad I wore it for you."

Zach told his wife that it was going to be OK. After the therapist and psychiatrist left the room, the security guard and Zach convinced Lisa to think of it as a vacation. When they said this, she was comforted. Boy, did she need a vacation! She had no idea that she was a 51/50, the code for being hospitalized for seventy-two hours because she was a danger to herself and others.

Lisa passed gas again openly and put her head on Zach's shoulder. As they waited for the paramedics to come to take her to the psychiatric hospital, they told the security guard how they met and got married. They had been young and in love. Justin, their firstborn, was the one who saved them. They had been going through some rough times, and after they had the baby, they waited until he was ten months old and then got married at the county clerk's office. An hour went by, and the paramedics came into the meeting room. The paramedic guy was Latino and very handsome.

"Are we ready?" he asked.

Lisa willingly sat on the gurney after she hugged Zachariah goodbye. They rolled her away, and she yelled out to Zach, "Remember. Concentrate," she said. She put up one finger and said, "Justin." She put up a second finger and said, "Joey." Joey was their second child. Finally, she put up a third finger and said their baby's name, "Zoey." He nodded and cried as they rolled her away. Lisa's heart was sad but only for a minute. As they rolled her away, she looked forward to her much-needed vacation. She thought this was all some sort of joke, and she was going to end up in Disneyland with her family.

Not a Vacation

As Lisa lay on the gurney in the back of the ambulance, the paramedic said, "I find it interesting how people can talk to spirits." She denied the whole idea; it was as though she'd turned on a switch to go back to the *normal* Lisa. They carried on a nice, small-talk sort of conversation.

"You smell good," Lisa said. It was a soapy scent. It almost permeated the whole ambulance.

"Thank you. I have to be clean for the work that I do," he said. His phone rang, but he didn't answer it.

"Someone is thinking about you and sending you positive energy," she said as though she were a wise old soul.

"I bet it's my wife because she just called," he said.

Lisa felt like an idiot. She was thinking that someone from his past was sending him positive energy, someone dead.

They rolled her into the hospital and into the main elevator. One of the paramedic guys, who happened to be

White, was prompted to do something work related, and he joked about it. "Sure, make the White guy do it."

Lisa sang in response, "White men! White men! White men! White men can't jump!"

She sat up on the gurney, and they thought she was probably nuts. But she was really sick with her illness, something she couldn't put a finger on at the moment. She stopped and told the paramedic gal that she reminded her of an old childhood friend. The paramedic thanked her but acted as though she didn't want to be in the same room as Lisa.

They rolled her onto the fourth floor, and she was still sitting up on the gurney. She stared at the White paramedic guy's name tag.

"Wow, this is a nice picture of you," she said.

He smiled at her as though he felt sorry for her. They took her off the gurney and escorted her to a chair. The paramedics left. A heavy-set woman approached her and took her shoelaces off, giving her two rubber bands to keep her shoes together. This was when she knew—this was no vacation.

Lisa remembered they took her shoelaces away when she was hospitalized at fourteen for psychosis and depression. What the hell, she thought to herself. But for a moment, she forgot where she was, and they took her to her room.

"Can I get some underwear?" she asked. She was bleeding from her period and needed sanitary pads immediately. "Also, can I get some shampoo, body wash, and lotion?"

The bald man smiled at her and said, "I'll see what I can find." He came back minutes later with the toiletries, and she was very grateful.

"Thank you so much."

He left the room and she walked into the restroom to take a shower. The water was so hot, and it dripped onto the floor outside of the shower curtain. She remembered her old host mother in Bath, England. Lisa had stayed in Bath for four months in college. The woman used to yell at Lisa, telling her to stop letting the water drip onto the floor while she was showering.

"I know you're in here, Carol. I'm trying, I'm trying!" she yelled. She thought she could feel her presence since she was dead, and Lisa laughed to herself. She started feeling again like she was being watched on a reality TV show and started beating on the shower walls with her knuckles in a rhythmic beat. She did that for several minutes then finished taking her shower. She walked out of her room and kept on walking. She walked through doors that buzzed at her, and she yelled, "Ahhh!" in shock. She noticed one of the staff ladies laughing nervously at her. Finally she found herself entering a room with a group of people, and in the center of the room was a mental health worker who was talking about medication, and Lisa yelled out of nowhere, "You're a crock of shit!"

One of the patients got pissed off at Lisa. "Why don't you let her finish talking?" he asked brashly.

Another patient started to badmouth the lady, and Lisa admired their team effort to bully her. Lisa stormed out of the room and one of the other mental health workers found her.

"Lisa, are you OK? Follow me, dear, it's going to be all right."

Lisa followed her into another room that had several chairs and one table.

She was gathering paperwork and had Lisa sign a whole mess of papers. Lisa paid attention to all the numbers in the dates and thought she had a special gift with the numbers, linking them to dates that she was a part of, dates that were painful to her. She thought she had the power to feel her pain. She also thought that she had undergone plastic surgery to disguise herself for a reason that only she knew. They finished the paperwork, and she went into her room to lie down for a bit. She was overwhelmed and also felt very cold.

Savior

About half an hour later, a mental health worker knocked at Lisa's door, the same one that was in the group, and she smiled at her.

"Your pastor is here to see you," she said.

Lisa thought that she was talking about some sort of pastor that visited the hospital from time to time, but he was the pastor of the church she belonged to. It was Pastor Mark. He came in smiling at her nervously. She didn't want him there at first, but minutes later, she felt comforted by his presence. He was a handsome man, forty, with red hair. As he looked at her, he noticed she was covered in blankets with only her head visible.

"Are you cold?" he asked.

Lisa nodded. "You know, you don't need to worry about me. All these people are so worried about me, but I'm fine," she said.

Earlier her father and her aunt had called to see why she was there and how she was doing. She was tired of all the phone calls and all the worrying.

"It's OK to worry about you because we all love you. You should let us worry. Do you want to pray?" Pastor Mark asked.

She nodded and he took her hand and held it. She rubbed his hand with her thumb as he prayed, and she felt a feeling of relief like she was going to be OK. He left shortly after he prayed, and she felt like she was some sort of savior. She walked down the hallway and heard a howling noise, which came from one of the patients. But she thought that people's sins were being revealed and that demons were coming out of all the people that were at that hospital. She thought she could fix this somehow. She was feeling so high and spiritual.

Allergic Reaction

That night Lisa tried to fall asleep after they had given her her medication. She noticed a mark on her hand that looked like a flea bite. She thought that it was from the medication they had just given her.

She marched over to the nurse's desk and yelled, "I'm having an allergic reaction to this medication!" The nurse looked at her hand.

"It'll be fine. Let me give you something for that hand," she said.

Lisa shut up for a moment. She hoped the mark was nothing, maybe just a flea bite. They gave her some other medication along with the creme.

"What is this?" she asked. She was paranoid.

They told her that it was Benadryl and that it was supposed to help her sleep. She was wondering if they were just telling her that. She went ahead and swallowed it anyway and went back to her room. It was Benadryl. They had given her all that they could give her, and Benadryl was her only option for the moment.

Sexually Harassed

Lisa woke up early the next morning, still not sure if she'd gotten any sleep, and walked out of her room and into the hallway. She saw the guy who had been bullying the mental health worker.

"Oh, Lisa! I dreamt that you were sitting on my face and told me not to stop. I went into your room last night and—."

She cut him off. "You what?"

"Don't worry. You were asleep. I didn't do anything."

She walked away from him. She thought she was hearing things. She didn't report this incident until after he left the hospital later that day. The social worker was so annoyed.

"That son of a bitch! He's in the right place now. He was harassing other women here. Next time, tell someone right away."

Lisa looked at her nametag; her name was Susan. Lisa told Susan that she thought she was hearing things and that her mind was playing tricks on her. That bastard had written his phone number on a newspaper and had given it to her. Susan threw it away.

Lisa apologized to Susan for the way she had acted the night before. She was in a better state of mind at the moment and knew that her behavior the night before was unacceptable. Susan accepted Lisa's apology and told her she understood and not to worry about it.

Butt Dance

Lisa ate breakfast in the main room. She was on a high and her breakfast was super delicious. The maple syrup tasted so sweet, just the right amount. She could smell the food, really smell the food, as though she were in the kitchen cooking it herself. It was so nice. The eggs were delicious, everything was just so yummy, and she could taste ten times more than usual. She felt the cold floor on her feet through the fuzzy hospital socks. She felt everything. Hot was extremely hot. Cold was so abrasively cold.

Before lunchtime, Lisa called her friend Fran. She came to visit right away. She came into Lisa's room, and Lisa told her the current diagnoses were postpartum depression and bipolar disorder, but Lisa was sure that was wrong as she wasn't feeling depressed at all. She just wanted to go home immediately. She tried playing the name game with Fran, the same one she'd played with the security guard back at the psychiatrist's office. Fran laughed nervously.

"Fran, I think my hands have a special healing power." Fran smiled.

"Oh yeah? Well, my shoulder is giving me problems."

She rubbed Fran's shoulder for a few seconds. An hour later Fran left. It had been so nice and comforting to see her.

Lisa was walking the hallway, just minding her own business, smiling at the cleaning lady. She approached her and smiled.

"You're not crazy," the lady said.

"I know," Lisa replied. She had her fooled. She was happy for the moment after her run-in with the cleaning lady and started doing the butt dance in the main room. The butt dance is when you wave your bottom in the air in a circular motion. She stopped after a bit, thinking what if there had been a camera watching her? She laughed hysterically and approached the nurse's station.

"I was just doing the butt dance in the main room. Are there cameras in there?" she asked. The bald man that had been there when she checked in laughed and said she was in luck. His name was Bruce.

"There are cameras in there, dear, but don't worry, they're not working right now, so let it rip!"

Lisa went back into the main room and continued to dance and sing. One of the other patients started playing the piano, and she stopped singing. She looked over her shoulder to watch her play, and her music put Lisa in a trance. She loved it. She suddenly started gazing off in the other direction and focused on the jigsaw puzzles on the shelf. She started to miss her family. It started to sink in that she wanted to be home desperately.

Pictures from Home

Bruce took Lisa's blood pressure, and she could smell his aftershave. It smelled nice and smooth, very comforting to her, a little soapy but not like hospital soap.

"You smell good."

"That means a lot coming from you. In this profession, we have to be clean." She loved him. Bruce was so adorable.

In the evening the patients were snacking on popcorn, which was considered a real treat around those parts. Lisa noticed one of the other patients was singing a Johnny Cash song.

"I'm gonna call you Johnny Cash," she said. He liked that.

Lisa made friends left and right. She had nicknames for everyone. The older woman in the wheelchair was Karen, so she called her Care Bear. Another man had a big belly and a voice like her father-in-law's; she called him Santa. There were a few others, and she felt like the popular kid in school.

Zachariah was able to visit Lisa the next day. She talked to him on the phone before he arrived and pleaded with him to bring her a picture of the kids and the college sweatshirt she loved to wear.

"Honey, you're not staying there that long. Why do you need your sweatshirt?" He sounded sad and she could tell he missed her.

"I'm just cold, honey. Bring me my jeans too." She needed those comforts.

Zach brought baby Zoey when he came to visit. "Honey, what did they say?" He looked at her with concern in his eyes.

Lisa told him she was probably going home soon after the seventy-two-hour hold. Susan, the mental health worker came to talk to them about bipolar disorder.

After she left the room, Zach had a few minutes left to visit with Lisa. She told her husband not to worry and that she would be coming home soon. She told him that Fran visited her and that everyone was so nice to her. She thanked him for the clothes and pictures. She knew the pictures from home would give her strength. One of the photos was of the three kids at Christmas time. They were posed in a row, on the couch. Zoey wore a little Santa hat and the boys had reindeer antlers on. She longed to hold all of them. She was so happy to see Zoey though. She was a bit worried that after seeing her, she would want to nurse. Luckily, that didn't happen. Zach had also given her a picture of just the two of them, him hugging her from behind. She wanted to cry. She said goodbye and told him not to worry. She was sure she would be going home once the seventy-two hours were up.

Lisa's mom and sisters came to visit her later that night. Sundee seemed so scared and confused. "See what happens when you get so stressed out?" she said, looking at Lisa with concern and frustration. Her sister Coco smiled at her nervously.

Her sister Shannen said, "You're fine. There are some strange people here. You don't belong here."

Lisa looked at all of them. All giddy, and in a weird and sly manner, she said, "But I am getting better." The visit was short; she hugged all of them. She assured her mother she would be going home soon. The next day, her seventy-two hours would be up.

The same day her mother and sisters came to visit her was the same day the guy she'd nicknamed Johnny Cash was released. She was going to miss him, as he often made her laugh during her stay. He was such a big guy. She stood on a chair and hugged him goodbye, tightly.

"It's not fair," she said.

"Take care of your baby," he said. He walked out of the room, and she cried for a little while.

Still Spinning

The psychiatrist was a good-looking man in his thirties. He told Lisa she should probably stay one more day. "There are certain risks that if you go home—" she cut him off.

"Risks? What kind of risks? Am I going to have a heart attack?" She was brash and gave him a stern look.

"No." He looked very frustrated with her and even rolled his eyes.

"OK then, I am fine." She was determined to get the hell out of there and get back to her family.

With a lot of hesitation, Dr. Gomez sent her home.

At home, Lisa was spinning. She was talking so fast. Her words went faster than her thoughts, so nothing she said made any sense. She was still on a high. Her mother-in-law phoned the patient coordinator for the outpatient program she was to attend. "Please help me," she said. She sounded so hopeless and worried. The patient coordinator asked Ore-Ida if she thought Lisa could sit through a group session. She told her yes, so the next day, Lisa attended one of the group sessions.

A lady named Clara met her. She was Asian and had on black pants, a colorful scarf, and a mismatched sweater. She wore glasses and seemed soft in her manners. She had a Chinese accent, but her English was great. She was a marriage and family therapist. Lisa immediately asked her to be her caseworker and the woman agreed, so she talked to Lisa about her progress.

In the group, Lisa ran into two buddies from the hospital. One of the ladies was gay and really liked her in a friendly sort of way. She said Lisa was adorable. The other was a gal her age who had been hospitalized for postpartum depression. She said she'd almost hurt her baby. Her hands would be doing one thing while her brain was telling her not to hurt her child. Lisa could tell this woman thought she was annoying. But she really was—Lisa's mania would take over, which made her hard to deal with.

The group session was interesting. The therapists taught the patients breathing exercises and techniques to help them with anxiety. Despite having laryngitis, Lisa asked a ton of questions and loved being the center of attention. Sadly, her voice was barely there but she still volunteered to dance while another patient played his keyboard. She didn't care what other people thought of her. Her dance moves were confusing, though, as she didn't have any actual rhythm. She just loved performing for the group during the break.

Her caseworker, Clara, was surprised when Lisa told her she sang and danced. Lisa's buddy from the hospital, the one with postpartum depression, said Lisa was a nut. She was a nut.

In one of the group sessions, Lisa did the butt dance again during one of the breaks. One of the other patients smiled at her, and she stopped.

"Continue," he said.

"Not if you're going to be uncomfortable," she said.

"No, I'm fine," he replied.

She decided not to continue. She was still on a high but was calming down just a little, just enough to not get sent home.

One of the patients was drawn to her. He was a hairy teenager and was all touchy-feely. She gave him a hug and told him he had pretty eyes. He responded with a smiling stare, and she immediately said, "I'm not coming onto you."

"I know," he said.

Another patient told Lisa of the first time an old man had jacked him off. She had no idea why he told her that little disgusting tidbit. She was grossed out by his disclosure and decided to stay away from him.

Vote Obama or Hilary

Lisa thought about particular moments in spurts. She couldn't stop thinking about these particular moments because her bipolar disorder didn't allow her to. She wished she could rewind time and fix everything. When she was in her mania, the psychosis took over. She truly lost touch with reality. She saw her husband bawling while she was at her highest of highs, and it didn't even faze her. She saw her six-year-old shaking with anxiety; he was just a normal six-year-old who shouldn't have felt that way, and she didn't even think to comfort him. She even thought the baby hated her.

They were so poor that they couldn't even afford to buy formula for the baby. She was so thankful for WIC (Women, Infants, and Children), a government program that aids people by providing them with nutritious food and formula for babies. She'd lied and told them she was being treated for postpartum depression. After all, that had been one of the first diagnoses. She had to stop nursing because of the medications. WIC gave her vouchers for formula but for a later date. Luckily, Sundee gave them a couple hundred dollars to hold them over.

Lisa asked her grandfather to help them, and he came through with five hundred dollars. They were two months behind with rent, but this money helped feed them in the meantime.

Zach and Lisa needed to go to the grocery store to buy a few things, and he told her to watch what she said to people. They went their separate ways in the store, and Lisa was talking nonstop about Barack Obama and Hilary Clinton. To every person she came across, she said, "Well, I hope you vote for Obama or for Hilary." She asked an older gentleman if he was voting for McCain, and he shook his head and said, "No, Hilary."

He probably thought she was insane. She would stop talking. She apologized to her pretty cashier friend and told her she was a bit speedy at the moment and that she would talk to her another time. Lisa was surely acting like her mother-in-law, Ore-Ida, had said: like she was on crack.

Back to the Drawing Board

In the outpatient program, the new psychiatrist assigned to Lisa realized she was on too low of a dosage of an antipsychotic. He put her on a much higher dosage and that seemed to do the trick for the moment.

But soon Lisa became overmedicated. At that time, from late January until about April, she couldn't feel emotions. Her mother-in-law said she was depressed, although Lisa would say she was numb. She couldn't even find it within herself to have fun on her son's seventh birthday. She tried though. She got the video camera and everything. She still wasn't herself.

Everything got better after a long down episode, which lasted for weeks. She felt whole again from May until November of that year, but then she was hospitalized for a second severe manic episode.

Lisa was going to perform in a concert in front of her Christian church, for fellowship. She was the lead singer for three songs. A couple of weeks before the concert, she sent out a mass email to all her friends and family, inviting them to the concert. She also outed herself as having bipolar disorder. She didn't hear back from most of the people. She started to lose sleep over it because she started to think that everyone didn't want to keep in contact with her since she was Christian and had bipolar. Her friend Ahmad was Muslim, and she adored him and his wife; she thought that she had offended him with the invitation because he didn't answer her mass email. She sent him an individual email that asked if he was avoiding her because of the whole Christian and bipolar thing. She thought that maybe he was annoyed by her invitation. Lisa cried the night that he didn't respond to her email. Her husband said to get it together, but she still lost sleep over it. She had always been so sensitive.

Lisa was about to perform on Friday night, but Zach saw something in her eyes, something not normal. When the bipolar would take over, he said that she would get a particular glare, almost as if she wasn't all there.

"Are you sure you're OK?" he asked.

She looked at him annoyed. "I'm just nervous, that's all."

The lights felt like little heaters against Lisa's skin. She felt so euphoric and spiritual. She prayed with her friend Amber in front of people at church, bowing their heads and all. Praying in public wasn't something Lisa would normally do. She was, for the most part, pretty discreet about praying.

Lisa performed and had a great time. But the audience's applause seemed like it was all fake, like she was on some fake TV show with fake people. After the concert, her spiritualness took over. She felt as though she had known her friend, Reba, the gal who was singing next to her, as a different person in her past.

"You remind me of someone," Lisa said. She was embracing her friend, and she felt as though they were experiencing a loss of some sort. She felt that she could sense the emotions of anyone who came near her.

Lisa praised the teenager who was singing on stage and talked to his mother. She couldn't stop talking and laughed so hard.

"Wow, he's good! I can't believe how good he is."

Lisa felt a weird connection with the teenager's mother as she had a daughter with autism. The girl was highly functioning but, still, a little off socially. Lisa felt as though she could feel her pain. It was so strange.

Lisa didn't sleep much that night or the next. She did something unusual; she listened to the radio and really focused on the lyrics. She had a sense that each word was connected to her life in some way, and she thought through music, she had all the answers.

"Honey, do you hear that? Listen to what I can do. I have a gift." He had heard her say that phrase before, from the last episode. "I can answer all your questions about life. Just listen to the next song."

No matter what song was playing, she thought she had the answers to fix people's problems. Her husband urged her to sleep. She took a nap and woke up feeling like she was a real angel. Zachariah called her Angel as a pet name, and her mother, Sundee, had let her borrow a book with an angel theme. Lisa thought Sundee was an angel too.

A fellow soccer mom had talked to Lisa about her baby who had died of SIDS. They had both agreed that this was her angel. She felt the urge to call her to tell her that her baby was OK and happy in heaven. She thought she could feel the baby's presence. Her mother-in-law hid her mobile phone and begged her not to call her, fearing she would embarrass her older son, who played soccer with the woman's son.

Ore-Ida became confrontational with Lisa and said, "I'm a lot bigger than you—."

Lisa cut her off. Lisa pushed her down onto the couch and was ready to fight. Zach begged Lisa to get some sleep. She went to her bedroom, sneaking her mobile phone in with her. She felt trapped in her own home and phoned her friend Fran. She let her know that everyone was acting foolish, thinking she was going crazy. She fell asleep then woke up and started to cry. Lisa felt spiritual again. This time she spoke Spanish and kept saying out loud, as if in prayer, to please forgive her family for they haven't done any wrong.

After her good cry, she started being manic again, laughing, crying, and just acting like a fool. Zach got the video camera and taped her laughing and also crying in frustration about her bipolar disorder.

She called her dear friend Tully, a fellow school mom.

"Wassup, Douglas? Where Tully at?" She was speaking as though she was in her teenage years when she tried to act stereotypically Black.

"Oh, hold on, Lisa." She sensed Douglas's confusion. He had never heard her talk like that before.

"Hello?" Tully said.

"What up, dog?"

"Who's this?"

"It's Lisa, who do you think it is?"

Tully chuckled nervously. "Oh, I didn't recognize your voice at first." She, like Douglas, had never heard her talk like that before and knew something was off.

"Tully, I think I might be having a manic episode. Everyone thinks I'm crazy," Lisa said.

"Do you want me to come over?"

"I don't know if you can handle seeing me like this."

"I'll be right over."

When she arrived, Lisa shouted, "Tully in the house!" Everyone had already eaten the dinner she'd prepared manically with her George Foreman Grill. "Tully, look at my Foreman Grill." She looked at Tully and started rapping. "Cause it's the lean, mean, fat-reducing, grilling machine. Yeah, it's the lean, mean, fat-reducing, grilling machine!"

Lisa performed a song for Tully with her mother-in-law in the living room. It was a song from the concert. Tully made fun of her ad-libbing in the song. Lisa stopped abruptly and whined and complained that she wasn't any good at singing. They looked at her with concern and told her she was pretty good and not to be ridiculous. Then Lisa showed Tully an old picture of herself.

"You're cute! Look at you and your fro," Tully said, smiling.

"It's ugly. I look terrible."

"No, you don't!"

"I'll be right back." Lisa went into the bathroom and overheard Zach telling Tully that she was talking to ghosts in the bathroom.

"I am not talking to ghosts, Zachariah! I'm talking to myself." She was a little annoyed.

She came out of the bathroom minutes later, and they all relaxed awhile with Tully. Before Tully left, Lisa asked her if she wanted some of Zach's birthday cake. His birthday had been a couple of days earlier. She argued with Tully about the size of the portion. Tully explained that her husband, Douglas, didn't like cake, so Lisa agreed that the portion was just right.

After Tully had left, Lisa put on a necklace with blinking lights that her sister had given her at the concert. It was one of those necklaces people would wear at nightclubs to get noticed.

Lisa started speaking Spanish to the El Salvadorian neighbors in their apartment complex. "Lo siento, lo siento," she said. That meant she was sorry, as her son kept running into their feet with his little Big Wheel. The mother said it was all right, and Lisa continued speaking Spanish, a language she was not fluent in. She went inside her apartment, and minutes later, she heard a knock on the door.

"Hi! We have chicken over here. Do you want some?" the neighbor boy asked.

"OK!" Lisa was ecstatic.

Zach asked her what she was doing next door, and she explained that William was making her a plate of food.

"Oh, dear," he said, rolling his eyes.

William brought the food to her. "Did your mom make this, William?" she asked.

"No, it's from El Pollo Loco."

Lisa's heart sank. She thought he was going to give her authentic El Salvadorian food. Oh well, she thought. She took the plate gladly and thanked William. He walked away, and she noticed he smelled nice.

"You smell good, William."

"It's my sister's perfume." He smiled.

"By the way, William, I like your Superman shirt."

He shook his head in response. "No, it's Soldier Boy," he said, grinning widely. He walked away. He was a good boy. Lisa felt a motherly love toward him.

She sat down with her plate after giving a couple of pieces of chicken to her boys. The chicken was absolutely delicious. She practically inhaled it. El Pollo Loco is the bomb diggity, after all, meaning that it was super good.

Zach and Lisa put the kids to bed. The almost four-year-old had a bit of a crying spell; Lisa hugged him tight and had a weird feeling. All of a sudden, she felt like her child was a special needs child and that she could relate to parents of children with special needs, such as kids with autism.

The boys went to bed, as well as her thirteen-month-old daughter. She tried watching *Family Guy* but couldn't concentrate. It was too much for her. She could feel her mania taking over, and she didn't want to speak.

"What's wrong honey?" Her husband was worried as hell, despite knowing she had a psychiatry appointment the next day.

She shook her head and started to play a game similar to charades. She pantomimed being stuck in a box.

"Lisa in a box!" he said.

She shook her head. She didn't have to make another gesture.

"Bipolar in a box!" he shouted.

She clapped her hands as she pointed to him in agreement.

He joked about the silent treatment. "I could get used to this," he said.

She finally started to talk after he pleaded with her to sleep.

"Honey, please get some sleep," he said.

"Honey, I need you to massage my feet," Lisa said.

"No, honey, just get some sleep!"

Lisa stood up, and he grabbed her by the wrists and slammed her down on the bed, or at least she thought he did.

"Ow!" she yelled. "You hurt me!"

"What do you mean?" he asked.

He truly wasn't trying to hurt her but was trying to get her to sit still and to get some sleep. He left the room for a minute, and Lisa dialed 911. She hung up immediately after it rang once. She started to get ready; she knew they'd come for her. She wore a hot-pink tank top under a brown blazer, jeans, and fuzzy, black slippers.

Five minutes later the police came, Zach asked Lisa if she had called the police and she told him she did. Lisa could hear the loud sound of the radio coming from one of the officer's belts. "Let's keep it down," she whispered. She didn't want them to wake up the neighbors. She looked at the redheaded police officer, who had a warm smile on her face. "I am having a manic episode, and I need a ride to the hospital," Lisa said plainly.

She requested to be driven to Million Oaks Hospital. She'd stayed there during her first episode. Her husband let them know they usually went to Kifer Hospital for emergencies, and they assured him that they would drive her to Kifer.

"Are you sure, honey? You need to go in tonight?" Zach asked.

"Yes, I'm sure." She felt it in her body. She really needed to get some help. A little part of her knew she wasn't herself. She hugged him tightly. "Bye honey, I love you." All she had with her was her purse.

"Now, for your safety, we're going to have to handcuff you," the redheaded police officer said.

"I would rather you not."

"This is for your safety."

Lisa complied, and they patted her down. She was very submissive that she seemed to be enjoying herself until the handcuffs started to hurt.

"Actually that's a little too tight. Can you loosen them just a little?" She could feel the hard cuffs against her wrist bones, and they hurt terribly. The officer loosened them, and she sighed with relief. In the car she started to freestyle rap, rhyming words she just spit out off the top of her head.

"I'm in the vehicle, going down Nimble Road, going to the hospital," she said, rapping. She felt like her style was smooth and that all the words rhymed. She stopped.

"Why did you stop? I was diggin' your rap there," the officer said.

"Thanks." Lisa continued rapping until they got to the hospital.

Lisa acted as though the officer was her friend. She brought Lisa into the ER and whispered something to the person at the front desk. The officer didn't say goodbye; she just disappeared. Lisa walked over to the security desk and sat on the counter, right at the guard's station. "No, no, you shouldn't sit there," one of the staff members said. A couple of other staff members told her to get down as well.

Lisa sat in the ER lobby and noticed two little boys, most likely brothers, sitting together with terrified looks. They were Latino, so she started with her Spanish again. "Tiene miedo?" She asked if they were scared. They nodded and asked why she was there. "I don't know," she said. Just then, the nurse called her name. She quickly went into the nurse's station and, through the window, waved goodbye to the brothers.

A nurse took her blood pressure, and as they were doing that, Lisa teased the other nurse and called him by his name as she'd noticed his nametag. He rolled his eyes and proceeded to help her onto a hospital bed.

A little later, she walked around the ER floor aimlessly. She noticed a nurse with an extremely crooked nose.

"Hey, why the hell is your nose like that?" She really wasn't in her right mind.

The nurse turned directly toward her. "Fuck you bitch!" She was livid.

Lisa immediately felt apologetic. She was wishing she could rewind time and not have said anything at all. She would never have done that in her normal state.

Lisa walked toward a blood pressure machine and started ripping it apart. She could not control her hands. Her hands continued to move, but she didn't agree with what they were doing. A whole bunch of pieces fell to the floor, and she got on her hands and knees, trying to pick up the pieces.

"It's OK, just go lie down," one of the doctors said.

A security guard came, and Lisa started throwing ice cubes at him. He caught each cube she threw, ninja-like, as if he were magic. They sedated her minutes later.

Lisa woke up, and two nurses were smiling at her. She sat up in the hospital bed. On her lap was a sandwich, and she chose not to say any words again.

She gestured a scissor motion with her hand on the sandwich, as if to say she only wanted half. They handed her the sandwich and said something to her in Tagalog, a Filipino language. She heard them say a familiar phrase, meaning *good evening*, and she immediately became alert.

"Where did you learn that?" Lisa asked.

"Oh, we learned it here at work," they replied.

She figured that with so many Filipinos in the nursing field, their coworkers were bound to know the language. As they situated her onto an ambulance gurney, she asked the nurses where she was going. They told her that she was going to Piedmont Hospital, which she wasn't familiar with at the time.

"I'd like to go to Million Oaks," she said.

"Where you go depends on how many beds they have available, dear," one of the nurses replied.

She nodded and waited for the paramedics to come. It was back to the drawing board.

Rosa Maria

Faces were changing. One person would be White, and then all of a sudden, they would morph into a person of color. Lisa was truly hallucinating.

"How did you do that? You just became Filipino," she said to a woman in the ER, the one who had helped transfer her into the ambulance.

"Yup, it just happened," she said. She may have been humoring her.

Finally the paramedics came, and she was a little anxious. Lisa was in the ambulance, rapping again. The words came out before her thoughts could form, so she wasn't making any sense, but at the time, she thought she was a genius at rhyming words. She talked about nonsensical things. She stopped minutes later and felt very spiritual again. She also felt like she could feel the paramedic's fear. She felt like she could look into his past and thought he had raped a woman. She started to gag, and her throat became extremely dry. They finally gave her water and brought her into the lobby of the hospital.

Lisa started spelling words in sign language, trying to talk to the female paramedic. She was gesturing cutting her tongue with scissors.

"No, no, you don't want to do that," they said.

She started to spell in sign language. B, I, P, O, L, A, R. But the female paramedic looked at her strangely.

"I don't speak sign language."

"Never mind," she said with frustration. For some reason, she couldn't verbalize *bipolar*. She was crying for help. In that second, she knew she was there because of bipolar disorder.

The next thing she remembered was running down the hallway naked, running away from one of the psychiatric hospital staff members. All of a sudden, he spoke Tagalog and demanded that she wear her hospital gown. She sort of woke up and did what she was told. One of the nurses, having seen her naked body, asked her if she worked out. She reminded Lisa of her landlady, Karen, and she needed that familiarity. She was just trying to calm her down. Lisa's body was far from in shape.

They stuck Lisa in what appeared to be some sort of group room. She sat there for a little while until she felt like she was being watched. She closed the curtains. She noticed a few games on one of the shelves; Jenga was one of them, a block-stacking game. She opened up the box and some blocks spilled out. She started to feel the blocks one by one as the sensation comforted her for whatever reason. Then she started stacking them to put them away.

Lisa started feeling spiritual again. She felt like she was an angel put on earth for a purpose. She still wasn't sure where she was though. A lady came and helped her fill out some paperwork. The next thing she knew, she was lying in bed while two staff members talked in Tagalog. It was dark, and she started drifting. She remembered feeling someone sitting at her bedside. It felt as though she were crying, feeling sorry for her.

Lisa woke up and noticed she was in a quiet room. She was lying in one bed while another lady was lying in a second bed.

"Where am I?" Lisa asked.

"You doooon't wanna knooooow," she said slowly with a low and raspy voice. She was a heavyset Latina woman in her fifties. She had curly hair.

"Really, where am I?"

"You dooon't waaanna knoooooow." The woman all of a sudden started to panic. "Nurse. I need my meds right this minute!"

She cried and Lisa hugged her tight. Her large bosom felt warm against Lisa's cold chest. Lisa hugged the woman's trembling body and felt such sympathy for her. She wanted to take the pain away. The nurse came and gave the woman her medications. She calmed down after a little while, but Lisa still wondered where the hell she was.

"What's your name?" Lisa asked her.

"Rosa Maria. You better take a shower and do your laundry, or you're gonna be stuck here longer. Show them you can be responsible, or they'll start taking your privileges away. You want to be on white sheet," she said.

What the hell was *white sheet*? Lisa would find out later.

After she showered, Lisa went to the group room and breakfast appeared in front of her, like magic. The place started to feel familiar, and she saw others in hospital gowns just like hers. Slowly she started to realize where she was. The nurse came by and gave her her meds.

After she did laundry, she was finally able to get back into her hot-pink tank top, jeans, and brown blazer. One of the hospital staff, a Black man in his early thirties, looked at her from head to toe and told her she looked nice.

Her breasts felt so heavy and droopy. She looked down and realized she wasn't wearing a bra. She walked to the front desk and demanded her bra back. The Black man who'd complimented her earlier looked at her with concern in his eyes.

"It'll be OK," he said. He walked through a door. Through a small window, she saw him approach a locker. He grabbed what looked like her bra and returned to the front desk. He started cutting it open to remove the underwire. Lisa was a little annoyed but happy to get her bra back. It was such a bittersweet feeling.

"Thank you so much!" she said.

Later on that day, Rosa Maria kept hounding her to get a Bible from the front desk.

"Get some shampoo and soap. Don't forget to ask for a Bible! Get your Bible!" She was so adamant that it scared Lisa a little.

Lisa got the Bible and started reading the Psalms. The words were so comforting. Green pastures, oh, how she wanted to be with her family in green pastures. Her heart ached.

White Sheet

"Brrrr-ack Obama rock, oh, rock Obama, baby!" Rosa Maria and Lisa were dancing in the hallway, and Emily, one of the staff, told them to be quiet.

"Whatever, Emily. You have a bad attitude!"

Emily rolled her eyes as Lisa started to stretch her legs on the floor. "You need to do that in your room!" she said.

So Lisa went to her room and stretched.

At dinner time, the dining area seemed so familiar to Lisa. It was like they'd decorated for Thanksgiving, with lots of oranges and browns. She knew then that she was at the same hospital they'd put her in when she was fourteen years old. Back then it used to be called CPC Piedmont. CPC stood for Community Psychiatric Center. Shit, she thought, somebody get me the hell out of here!

Lisa saw Juanito, the Filipino guy that told her to put her gown on after being foolishly naked.

"What happened last night?" she asked.

He laughed and told the other staff members in Tagalog that she got naked. It was as though he were a close cousin because it didn't bother her at the time that he took her nakedness lightly. She was sure he'd seen plenty of nakedness in his line of work.

Lisa was at dinner with a few strangers. She listened in on one particular conversation.

"Once you're on white sheet for a couple days, you move to the third floor. People are more laid back there, and we play poker," one young man explained. He was an attractive man in his late twenties. His hair was a tad messy, but it went with his T-shirt and jeans.

"I want to play poker. How do I get there?" Lisa asked.

"Just listen to what they say, be on white sheet for a couple days, and you get to move."

Part of her wanted to move to the third floor where she thought all the *normal* people were. A certain feeling tugged at her heart. She became extremely homesick. She was going to do everything right. She needed to go to the groups, take her meds, and participate in the activities.

They got to do crafts, sing karaoke, and play games. In the midst of all the activities, Lisa thought of her family. She kept asking for her assigned psychiatrist. She asked herself where in the fuck was she anyway. The second time she saw her psychiatrist, Lisa made the mistake of telling her she was hearing things. For instance, a patient would converse with her, and Lisa would hear different words coming from their mouths as they talked. The psychiatrist upped the dosage of one of the meds, and the confession may have cost her an extra day at the hospital.

Lisa asked for a representative so that she could get a hearing to be able to go home sooner. She felt trapped. Her rep came to talk with her and told her she would have a hearing in a couple of days.

Zach came to visit her on the third day. This time, at this particular hospital, children were not allowed. They went into a small meeting room with a desk and three chairs.

"What did they say? Are you coming home soon?" he asked.

"I hope so. I haven't seen the doctor yet, but I think I'm getting close. I miss you guys so much. How is everybody? Are the kids OK?"

"Don't worry about the kids. Worry about getting better so you can come home."

Lisa wanted to cry, but the tears never came. The goodbye was difficult.

She officially won her hearing and they released her the same day. Her husband and three children waited for her in the downstairs lobby. She had her family back. She was victorious! She had been on white sheet for a couple days but never moved to the third floor. She didn't care. She was going home. After five days of hell, she was going home.

Bipolar Does Not Define Her

Lisa's family and friends checked in with her every once in a while. For instance, she would be talking pretty fast on the phone with her friend Tully, and Tully would ask, "Are you OK? You're talking fast right now." And Lisa would reply. "I'm OK but thank you for noticing." That helped her.

The question "Are you OK?" sometimes annoyed her. One evening, she was really immersed in scrapbooking in her six-year-old's book, and her daughter placed a Santa hat on her head. Lisa completely forgot about it and came into the living room, still focused on her scrapbook.

"Are you OK?" Zachariah asked.

"Why do you ask?" She was slightly annoyed.

"You have a Santa hat on, and it's not Christmas."

"I'm fine. I forgot that Zoey put this on my head." She chuckled but was still a little frustrated by the situation.

One night her mom and her mom's boyfriend took Lisa and Zach to a comedy show, and Lisa laughed, as anyone at a comedy show would. The next day her mom phoned her.

"Are you sick?" she asked.

"No, I'm fine."

"OK, I just wanted to say hi."

The question bothered Lisa over the next couple of days, so she called her mom and asked her why she wondered if she was sick. Her mom said she'd noticed her laughing pretty hard, but that it was probably because of the comedian. Lisa got off the phone with her and was a little disturbed by the call.

Sometimes, it felt as though people were starting to watch her every move, afraid she might flip out. The other day, Lisa told Zach she needed to take some medication for her anxiety, and he said he needed her not to flip out. He explained he needed his hernia surgery and she needed to be there for the kids. She assured him that she would be fine. Her mother-in-law asked Zach if he thought Lisa was going to have a manic episode, saying that she hadn't seen the apartment as messy as it was in a long time. Lisa called her back, insulted, and told her that everything was fine.

Lisa took it one day at a time and she felt blessed that she had three wonderful kids to keep her vigilant about her bipolar disorder. She knew that she had to let her family and friends worry. They sort of held her accountable. She knew that she had to let them ask a question when they felt something was off. But they also needed to know that she would be fine. A certain behavior that was out of the ordinary wasn't always because she had bipolar disorder. She was holding herself accountable as well.

Free Sex

Back when she was nineteen years old, Lisa became promiscuous. She left home because she needed the freedom. She didn't want to follow any parent's rules. She wanted to be free, and the promiscuity made her feel freer.

She had a boyfriend at that time; Drew was manipulative and jealous. She told him she had cheated on him with several men, and he flipped out.

"You fucking bitch! How could you do this to me?"

They worked that problem out, but she cheated again. That time, he told her that he loved her unconditionally and thought it was OK. She left because she knew it wasn't meant to be.

Lisa talked to Drew years later and let him know she'd since been diagnosed with bipolar disorder.

"That explains a lot. I knew there was something wrong, but I didn't quite know what it was. Thanks for telling me."

Lisa experienced a common symptom of a bipolar manic episode—an increased sex drive. Lisa called singles' phone lines to look for men to have free sex with; she purposely made her voice sound sexier. She met the men at restaurants, and they would end up at his place or a hotel. She couldn't get enough sex. She wanted it more and more each day. She felt so enthralled with and needed by these men. They made her feel pretty for a mere few hours, but at the end of the day, she felt so used up. One man in San Francisco told her that she should lose fifteen pounds. She started to feel more uncomfortable with her body but still wanted more sex. She would stay up at night and fantasize about her next encounter. It was as though she couldn't sleep until she fulfilled that need.

One man met her, took one look at her, and told her she shouldn't be meeting men on this phone line. She woke up to the fact that she was so very ashamed of herself. She thought of all the times she'd had sex with various men and wanted to throw up. She blamed herself, not bipolar, but perhaps if she were treated, she wouldn't have such sexual energy.

Zachariah

Lisa had met her husband, Zachariah, shortly after she'd broken up with Drew. Zach was a cute White guy with a goatee. He was so charming. They fell in love immediately, although he didn't kiss her until their tenth date. After Zach and she took a trip to Las Vegas, a trip Drew was supposed to take her on, Drew asked her to marry him. She thought that was pathetic. She told him no and that she was truly in love with Zach.

Six months after Zach and Lisa met, she got pregnant with their first child. They had a rocky first couple of years. They would fight so much, and she would scream at him. A couple of times, Lisa held a knife to her body, threatening to kill herself.

"You need help," Zach said.

Lisa wanted attention. She was needy and jealous. While attending a wedding, they saw his ex-girlfriend who had just found out that Zach and Lisa had gotten married.

She looked at Lisa and said, "He didn't get my permission."

Lisa flipped out, and Zach and she had a huge fight. He threw his wedding ring across a hotel meeting room. He had been drinking. They left the wedding and continued to fight.

One night Lisa found out that Zach had been doing crank for months. She knew something was off when she found him awake at 4:00 a.m., that's when he came clean to her about it.

"What's wrong? Tell me."

He looked at her and started crying.

"I've been doing crank behind your back for months now," he said.

"I'm done with you." She was ready to leave him. She didn't want Justin to be around drugs while growing up.

They called Zach's mother, and she diffused the situation somewhat. They were so close to breaking up, but they hung on and they worked it out.

Lisa thanked her lucky stars for him. He was her rock. They stuck by each other through so much. She'd thought he would leave her after her first manic episode, but he'd hung on for the ride.

When Lisa laughed alone in her mania, he stood by her and took care of the children. When she cried alone in her depression, he tried to make her smile. She didn't know what she would do without him. He was her soulmate.

Three children later, they lived life day by day. They used to worry about being able to pay rent sometimes, but the bottom line was they loved each other no matter what.

Paranoid

When Lisa was in a manic state, she felt so high, like she could do anything in the world. When she started to spiral, she would focus on specific phrases like "be aware of your surroundings."

During her first manic episode, Lisa felt so paranoid. She thought that someone was going to take her children away. She didn't know who would take them away, but nonetheless, she focused on keeping them safe with her. She locked the door constantly. She was furious when Justin's school called; they were concerned that he missed several days of school. Her mother-in-law, Ore-Ida, was looking for the doctor's note, and Lisa saw a pen in her hand.

"Don't you try to change the dates on that doctor's note!" Lisa screamed.

Then Lisa snapped at the school secretary over the phone.

"Don't you have a mother?" she asked her.

She said yes, even though that had nothing to do with the situation. Lisa hung up. She wasn't making any sense at all.

Her mother-in-law called the secretary back and apologized to her, telling her that Lisa wasn't quite herself. Ore-Ida faxed over the doctor's note as Lisa feared *they* would take him away from her. *They* were her biggest fear.

She noticed her neighbor next door and a police car in her parking space.

At first, she'd thought that the police were there for her but then realized they were there for the neighbor. "If you need any help, let us know," Lisa told her.

Bullied

From the beginning, Lisa had gone to private school from kindergarten through ninth grade but had decided to try public school for sixth grade. She wanted to see what public school was like. It would be an adventure. She wanted to be popular, so she made sure she hung out with all the popular kids. She had a nice Vietnamese friend Ly Tran, who adored Lisa. Ly loved how Lisa dressed, and Ly kept her company, although Lisa found other friends who caused her more trouble than anything.

One day Lisa went to her friend Maria's apartment without her mother knowing. The next day Maria accused Lisa of stealing one hundred dollars from her place. Maria's girlfriends Elise and Marge accused her as well, and they hadn't even been there. Maria must have told them that Lisa did it. Other girls had been there, too, but all their fingers pointed to Lisa, the little private-school girl with a new pair of shoes and a matching bag. Elise Cook and Marge Diaz made her life hell. They would bump into her harshly with their boney shoulders. Elise slapped her grubby hand onto Lisa's desk and said coldly, "You better give that money back to Maria, or else!"

Lisa didn't talk to her parents for days or eat much. Her mother asked her what was wrong, and Lisa confessed to her what was going on. Sundee taught her how to fight; she pushed her down onto the floor.

"Now get up! Fight back!" she yelled.

They did a few drills and she told Lisa to go back to school, ready to fight. She went back to school after that and told Marge to meet her after school. Marge cried and there was no meeting after school. Nonetheless Sundee was tired of the bullying and transferred Lisa to a school near her grandparents' house.

Lisa wanted to be popular again. She hung out with all the cool kids. This time she didn't get bullied. She was well-liked by her peers. She stuffed her bra to get noticed by the boys. She did want to fit in. All the girls wore makeup; Lisa would put makeup on at school so her mother wouldn't find out. When her dad picked her up, he usually let her wash it off at a nearby gas station. One day she went home, but she hadn't quite gotten the eyeliner washed off and tried to hide her eyes. Her mother was furious. Lisa didn't wear makeup again until her sophomore year of high school.

Her mother was there when she needed her. She'd protected her from Elise Cook and Marge Diaz. She'd even gone to Marge's house and had a talk with her mom and sisters. She had diffused that situation. Her mother took care of Lisa when she was sick, both before and after her very first hospitalization.

Weird Child

Lisa had been a weird kid. In kindergarten, she'd gotten in trouble for bothering her friend Penny. What the teacher hadn't known was that Lisa was trying to smell Penny's armpit, which smelled of fresh baby powder. Lisa loved the way things smelled. She especially loved the way her mother smelled, a light perfume that comforted her.

At five years old, Lisa didn't know about sex yet, but she had urges to rub herself *down there* against doors in her apartment. She rubbed until she felt somewhat of an explosion down there. She couldn't explain it at the time, but it felt so good to her five-year-old body. As an adult Lisa wondered if it could have been due to bipolar energy. Perhaps. She would never know, but she was glad that she was getting treated for this illness now.

As a child Lisa was always so sensitive. One snap from her mother or father resulted in her crying. She was also a pain in the ass. If a taco shell broke, she would cry for a new one, and without hesitation, her mother accommodated her by giving her a new shell.

One day Lisa and her mother were cuddling on the couch, and Lisa had a sudden urge to squeeze her mother's face and scream very loudly. Shocked, her mother sat there with a worried look on her face. Lisa calmed down after a few minutes and acted as though nothing ever happened. Lisa and Sundee will never forget that day.

Justin

Justin, Lisa's firstborn, had been affected by her first manic episode. He'd been almost seven years old and experienced a great deal for a child. While she was pregnant, her husband was having issues with work and anxiety, possibly a bit of depression. He started going to the local bar immediately after his workday ended. Lisa was so frustrated and tried many times to get him to leave the bar, but he was so stubborn and stayed. One day his own mother tried to take him out of the bar, and he told her to leave him the fuck alone. Lisa kept in touch with the bartender; one night she told Lisa that if she didn't come to pick him up, she would call him a cab because he'd fallen asleep at the bar. He eventually came home on foot.

One night Zach and Lisa had a fight, and she begged him to come home, but he wouldn't, even though it was a work night. She decided she would sleep in the boys' room as she was so furiously angry with Zach. She heard him come through the door hours later. She waited several minutes then went to the bathroom and found a bloody towel on the floor. She started to panic and entered their bedroom quickly.

"What happened?" She was almost crying by this time, as Zach's head was horrifically bruised.

"I got jumped," he said.

Zach told her about five men at the bar who had been talking about football; they all jumped him, although only two or three of them actually beat on him. He heard one of the men say he was going to get his knife out to use it on him, and that was about all he remembered. But one man told him not to bother. Thank God for that night; it was a wake-up call for him. He stopped going to the bar after that incident.

Justin was shocked by what had happened to his father. He thought his father was so invincible, like Spiderman. Once he saw this all unfold, he became such a worrier. He had terrible anxiety and couldn't focus on school. And then his world turned again when he saw his mother go through her manic episode.

Justin saw her singing out loud for all the neighbors to hear; she banged the dresser in the bedroom to a certain rhythm; she spanked him on the leg once.

"Why did I do that?" she asked herself out loud.

"Because you have issues," he replied.

He was so smart for his age and so innocent, yet here he was with two parents he thought could flip out again at any time. After Lisa's second manic episode, which was ten months after the first one, he was so devastated that it had happened again. That was years ago, and as a teen, Justin was now doing better. He worried about Lisa from time to time but for the most part, he thought she would be fine from now on. He had a good heart and was very sensitive. Lisa loved him so much and hoped he knew that she would take care of herself for their family.

Justin's First Manic Episode

Justin was seventeen years old. He wasn't sleeping much. For two nights, he was on his phone rapping along to rap music, freestyling nonsensical things. Lisa took him to school against her better judgment.

Lisa was substitute teaching for a third-grade class when she received a phone call from the high school. The vice principal told her that Justin had called a female student the *B* word; she knew this was so unlike him. She also said to Lisa, "From mom to mom, it seems as though he has had like ten Red Bulls."

Lisa apologized for her son's behavior but also told the vice principal that she thought he might be having a manic episode. Her mother-in-law picked him up and took him home. Lisa left her job early, went straight home, and then took Justin to the ER, where she knew he would get help, get something. She didn't want it to escalate. She knew if they didn't intervene now, he would get worse.

He was pleasant but very hyper, talking to everyone he saw in the ER. Lisa kept apologizing for him because he was coming off as very rude in some instances. An older black woman approached her and told her that she shouldn't apologize for him, that he was in a safe place where people understood why he was there. She also said that her own son was just like him. Lisa thanked her.

Justin kept looking at Lisa and said loudly, "Ma, you're the one that should be here, not me. You're the bipolar one." He was frustrated and tired of waiting. He was rapping again in the ER lobby. Lisa's mother-in-law, who had come with them, told him to stop. She told him so loudly that one of the nurses yelled at her to stop instigating the situation, as she was making it worse. Zach came a bit later. Justin, at this point, was combative and told his parents to leave him alone. He stepped outside.

Zach followed him out and said, "Justin, you have to go into the hospital right now, because you're not yourself."

Justin yelled, "I'm fine, nigga!" He postured toward Zach and said, "Leave me alone, nigga! I'm fine!"

Zach, at this point, talked to one of the security guards to help him get Justin inside.

One of the security guards, said matter-of-factly, "We can't lay our hands on him because he hasn't been admitted to the hospital yet."

Justin's First Manic Episode

Zach said, "I am going to call the cops then, so he'll go."

The security guard said, "I'll be right back." About two minutes later, the security guard came back. "OK, so it's a different story now. Now that he's been admitted as a patient, we can handle him."

Lisa was relieved that they didn't have to involve the police. Justin followed the security guard, and he became less aggressive; still very hyper but pleasant as well.

He stayed in an ER bed in the hallway for two days. No room, just a bed. Lisa and Zach were frustrated and prayed he would be admitted to the local psychiatric hospital. Hospital staff told them that pediatric beds were hard to come by and that Justin might have to go to the Bay Area, where they would have to drive almost three hours to visit him. Lisa prayed hard and Justin did get into the local psychiatric hospital.

After his first day, the hospital staff told Lisa that he was very pleasant but wouldn't go to sleep. This sounded very familiar to her because she had been in this position years ago. They gave him a journal; he asked for a second one and then a third one. He was writing rhymes just like Lisa had done when she was fourteen years old.

Zach and Lisa visited him as soon as they could. He asked to come home and said he wasn't even sure why he was in there. They found out he had THC (the active ingredient in cannabis) and Adderall in his system;

he'd gotten into Zach's Adderall. Justin apologized and begged to come home. Every time they came to visit, he would be so upset because they weren't taking him home. On one visit, Lisa came with her mother-in-law, and Justin said that if they weren't taking him home that they should just leave. Lisa understood his pain.

Jed, a close of friend of Justin's, came with Zach and Lisa to visit him, but Justin was asleep when they arrived. They decided they shouldn't wake him as he hadn't slept for days. The next day, Justin called Lisa, crying. He thought Jed had died. She reassured him that Jed was fine and that he'd even come to visit him. Justin calmed down after a little while and hung up.

In the second week, he still wasn't sleeping very much. He wasn't cleaning himself well either. He had huge flakes of dandruff in his hair, and his lips were extremely chapped. Zach and Lisa went to visit him one day, and they found him in the quiet room. He pretty much took over the room, screaming, "NO! I see the blood! I see the blood!"

Zach grabbed him and said, "There's no blood, Justin. You're seeing things. It's OK." He hugged him, and then they got a pizza for him. They'd learned he wasn't eating anything there, so they were allowed to bring him his favorite foods and snacks. Justin said all the hospital food was poisonous. He also kept telling them he was famous and had to record his music. He was so frustrated that he couldn't go home. He hit a couple of staff members,—one girl on the forehead and another on the back of the head. Lisa apologized to the young woman, who looked at her, smiled, and said, "It didn't hurt." She was an angel.

The doctor told Zach and Lisa that Justin had climbed over the counter in the day room and that he was very combative, but that Justin enjoyed playing music in his studio. The staff was ordered to inject Justin with Benadryl and Thorazine every time he became aggressive. After several medication changes, he finally responded to a couple that worked well. By the third week, his aggression subsided.

Justin came home after three weeks but was still fragile. His parents had to watch his every move, but he took his medications every day without a fight. He started to lose his beautiful hair, a side effect of one of his medications. The doctor lowered the dosage and gave him vitamins to combat the hair loss.

He felt that his whole summer sucked. He was about to be a senior in high school, and he had to go through all this pain. Lisa and Zach planned a restful summer for Justin by taking good care of him, giving him his meds, and making sure he got some sleep each night. Friends came over sometimes to visit. But Justin never remembered any of that summer.

Justin's Second Episode

For the first quarter of his senior year, Justin went through home studies. One of the teachers from his high school visited once a week to teach him lessons and collect the week's work. He was doing so well until he went to the powderpuff game at school with friends. It was October. "Can I go to the powder puff game with my buddies?" he asked. "You can go but mom is going to have to go with you," Zach said.

Lisa gave him space at the game. She sat up top in the bleachers as she watched him enjoy his time with his friends. Jed was there, as well as Ricky. When it was time to go home, Justin lost sight of his mother in the crowd. He looked around but couldn't see her and he got anxious. He found her and then agreed to meet her in the parking lot in the van. If she could rewind time, she would have done things differently—she would have guided him to the van in the parking lot and then taken him straight home. Instead, she had Jed lead him to the van. They saw a similar van in the parking lot and headed toward it; Lisa saw them and got out of the van and yelled to them so that they could see where she was. Justin got in the van, looking like he had seen a dead body. He was so glad they were going home.

Justin didn't sleep for three nights, and one morning at about 4:00 a.m., he ran around the house with his football under his arm, screaming nonsensical things. Later that morning he was punching his brother Joey angrily, and Lisa had to tackle him to the ground so he would stop. Zach and Lisa were already trying to prolong his stay home and avoided taking him to the hospital. They even went through an emergency checklist to make sure he didn't need to be admitted to the hospital. He passed the test. However, the next day Justin was talking to their dog and pet bird as though they could understand him. He was not in his right mind again.

In the ER, Lisa and Zach prayed so hard that he would go back to the local psychiatric hospital where he'd stayed before and that the angels would watch over him that night. He was admitted to the psychiatric hospital, and one of the workers asked why he was there again. The hospital workers were angels; they cared for him so lovingly. A few of the nurses would even rub his back until he fell asleep.

Lisa's cousin and one of her sisters visited him and cried after the visit because they saw how debilitating this was for Justin. He begged them to get him out of there. Again he was so frustrated with this stay. Zach's cousin visited, and Justin begged him to get him out of there. He was even there for Halloween, but thankfully, he had candy.

One time around one in the morning, the psychiatric hospital called Lisa to tell her that they had to take Justin to the ER at the hospital across the street. Zach and Lisa rushed to see him. He was throwing up, and the doctors weren't sure what was going on because he had a fever. Justin had been on medication that was a last resort since he hadn't responded to most of the other meds. So Lisa and Zach decided to take him off that medication and put him back on the other ones. He had already stayed at the hospital for three weeks. They felt so helpless, and Justin was as paranoid as hell. He was admitted to the intensive care unit and kept there for two days. The doctors were just about to send him back to the psych hospital, but Zach was adamant that they send him home. Lisa cried and begged her husband to make him go back to the psych hospital, but Zach said they were taking their son home to care for him themselves.

A few months later, Justin fell hard for a girl. He started to get manic again after they broke up. He started back on medication after having stopped all meds for about a year. He ended up in the hospital for four days after trying to hurt himself. He came home a little too early.

Justin's Second Episode

Zach and Lisa were very emotional at his high school graduation. They just hoped he could thrive and be happy. That's all they really wanted for him. He tried community college for a day but came home, realizing it was too soon to go right into school. He needed more time to heal.

Whenever Justin was in the hospital, Zach and Lisa had such a difficult time coping. Home wasn't the same without him. Lisa and Zach talked about their memories of when Justin was younger and how smart and cute he was. He was and continued to be a beautiful person.

Joey

Joey loved his brother intensely. He watched him closely too. One day, the family was agreeing that Justin was a bit manic. So Justin was very lucky to have family to watch out for him, making sure he was healthy and most importantly, making sure he got the sleep he needed.

One evening Joey scared the hell out of Lisa. He had football conditioning in the weight room at school and told her he'd call her when he was finished. By five o'clock, she hadn't heard from him. Her mind was racing, thinking of the horrific things that could have happened to him. He was a strong and tough boy but very slender, weighing 125 pounds.

She drove to the high school and waited for fifteen minutes in the front where she usually picked him up. Still, nothing. She walked around campus, looking for him, not caring if she embarrassed him. She asked his band buddies if they had seen him, and they said they hadn't.

Lisa drove home, frantically looking for him on the streets where she thought he might be. Still, nothing. She called Zach, and he told her Joey was home. She screamed on the phone and drove home as fast as she could.

Lisa approached her son and hugged him so tight. She thought he would flinch, but he returned the hug as she cried so hard.

"You scared me, Joey. I was thinking of all the bad things that could've happened to you. Next time, call me. And if your phone is dead, leave a voicemail from a friend's phone."

He agreed but told her she should've known he'd be all right to find his own way home.

The next day Joey told Lisa he was stressing out about the way she'd acted. He was hinting at her mental illness.

"Joey, when you have kids of your own someday, you'll understand. I'm a mom. That's what moms do."

He smiled and told her not to worry about him.

Joey was a talented drummer and athlete who loved football and lived life as a teenager should. He learned about bipolar disorder from watching his mother and brother. His parents were very proud of him and hoped he would lead a healthy and productive life.

Zoey

Zoey was beautiful, smart, funny, the list goes on. She was a wonderful dancer and artist. But Lisa and Zach worried about her. She had trichotillomania, a condition which causes her to constantly and excessively pull her hair out, one by one, strand by strand. It started when Justin was hospitalized the first time around.

Zoey was Lisa's anchor before her first manic episode. Zoey needed Lisa to nurse her, and she did. She needed Lisa's presence, and she was there. Zoey was three months old during Lisa's first manic episode and one year old during her second manic episode. Lisa knew Zoey loved and accepted her, and Justin too.

Zoey Hid the Zap!

Lisa was becoming hypomanic again. She was drinking Zap, an energy drink with three hundred milligrams of caffeine. She was supposed to take Zoey to a concert for her fifteenth birthday, but Zachariah said if Lisa was still hypomanic, they couldn't go. Lisa was talking to everybody again—the workers at Starbucks and the staff at any grocery store where she shopped. She couldn't stop laughing either. Zoey realized one day that her mother was drinking energy drinks.

"Ma, you cannot drink these energy drinks. That is why you're manic!"

Lisa said, "Zoey, I'm *hypo*manic. There is a difference."

Zoey hid all the energy drinks that were in the fridge. Zach needed his own drinks, but Lisa forgot to buy them for him. She offered him one of hers, but Zoey had hidden all of them. She asked Zoey to give her one to give to Zach.

Her dad confirmed the drink was for him, but Zoey didn't give her mother the drink; instead, she waited until her dad came home and handed it to him directly, so Lisa wasn't able to get ahold of any energy drinks. Zoey looked after her like a parent. She really wanted to go to the concert, so Lisa decided to cut out all caffeine a week before the concert. She finally mellowed out in time for the special day with Zoey. They would have so much fun. Zoey told her mother not to talk to strangers; she didn't want to be embarrassed, because Lisa sometimes put her foot in her mouth without meaning to. They had a fantastic time at the concert. Lisa was centered in. She was going to be all right.

Rina Swiveler

Lisa was jealous at times, in an unhealthy way. When he was in high school, Zach's best friend Brad Woods died in a horrific car accident. Zach felt he needed to take care of Brad's girlfriend, Rina Swiveler, and they became best friends. After a couple of years, the relationship developed into a love affair. He had loved her dearly, but after high school, they'd drifted apart. Then years later, through social media, they found each other and started talking by telephone. They shared a long history and he loved Rina dearly.

Lisa was all right with the friendship at first, until their minutes on the phone became hours. Lisa was curious. What could they be talking about? Reminiscing about old times? After all, Rina was attractive. Lisa was so jealous that she tried to figure out the password on Zach's mobile phone; it locked after several attempts. She threw the phone on the ground and cracked the screen. Lying to Zach, she said that she had dropped the phone.

He was so livid. He knew she was lying and wouldn't forgive her for several days. She didn't think she was the one in the wrong. She asked him why they needed hours to talk, why so long? He told her they talked about old mutual friends. They had both lead interesting lives; they had both been young and on drugs. He'd left his town to live with extended family after being up to no good.

He told Lisa she had better stop being so insecure and obsessive and asked if it could be her hypomania. But she didn't want to blame her jealousy on bipolar disorder.

Ore-Ida sent Rina a nasty email telling her to leave Zach alone. Rina wrote back, putting Ore-Ida in her place; she said Ore-Ida was horrible to even mistrust her son and cause trouble between Zach and Lisa. Lisa, after several days, got over her jealousy and eventually became good friends with Rina. Rina had a good heart and meant no harm. She had a happy marriage and children of her own. She was even there for the manic ride that happened around Christmas thirteen years after Lisa's last hospitalization.

The Switchover

Lisa was tired of her pregnant-looking belly, so she talked to her psychiatrist about switching over to different meds. She wanted so terribly to be slender again, like how she was before her babies. Dr. Ted Baxter was an attractive man, small in stature but tall in character. He was confident and also very sarcastic. Lisa was adamant that she wanted to switch over to something else. He gave her the OK, and she started to taper down on her main medication. She felt a little off but fantastic; she felt so high, like she could do anything. She cooked carefully and paid attention to her ingredients. She made French toast, sprinkling on cinnamon and brown sugar, then frying the battered bread in wonderful butter. She felt she was on top of the world.

It was Joey's seventeenth birthday. Lisa was compelled to get the kids Slurpees as they rode in the van while Joey's favorite Christmas radio station played. On the way to get the Slurpees, they spotted Joey's bandmates in a grocery store parking lot.

Lisa honked and yelled, "It's Joey's birthday!"

They all smiled and said, "We love you, Joey!"

He was so embarrassed and annoyed. "Ma, why did you do that?" He was not amused.

Lisa stopped at a gas station to get the kids Slurpees. Despite the COVID pandemic, the store workers were not wearing masks. Lisa felt a little annoyed and obnoxiously asked, "So do I have to wear a mask? I mean, you both aren't. So do I?"

Giving her a puzzled look, one worker said, "It's your choice."

She bought the Slurpees and some cigarettes for Zach. She overheard a man telling the worker he wanted to quit smoking.

"Please quit. Life is too short," she said, looking at him with concern in her eyes.

He nodded and smiled at her nervously. "I'll try."

She walked out of the store and saw a young man who looked about twelve years old pumping gas.

"Are you old enough to drive, buddy? You seem a little young."

He told her he was sixteen years old and a good driver.

"OK." As she walked away, she rolled her eyes. She felt so high like she was so important to the world. She was going to save the world somehow. Her medicine switchover was happening, but she failed to take a higher dose of the new medicine as she tapered off the old medicine. She felt so good, she thought her meds were perfect.

Laughing and Crying Alone

Bawling at Walgreens

Ore-Ida was acting like she was going to have another TIA (transient ischemic attack), or ministroke, and Lisa demanded Zach purchase a blood pressure monitor to take her blood pressure. Money was tight for all of them, but after pleading, Lisa got her way, so she and Zach drove to Walgreens with Justin. She felt so high like nothing could get in her way. Zach was extremely annoyed with her. She saw a toy as they were in line to buy the blood pressure monitor; it was one of those toys that had rubber bubbles to fidget with, popping them back and forth.

"Can I get this?" She looked at Zach.

He annoyingly told her no, and she bawled so loudly that the people in the store were staring at her in shock.

"I want it! I want it!" She cried and screamed.

He said, "Fine! Now, go to the van!"

He handed her the keys, and she walked out quickly and got to the van. All of a sudden, the van alarm went off, startling her. She started banging on the van windows on the outside and yelling for help, but no one came. Finally Zach and Justin came out, and seeing her in such a manic state, Justin threatened to call the police. She begged him not to. Zach told her she needed to calm down and come back into the store to pay for the blood pressure machine because only she knew Ore-Ida's pin number. They walked back into Walgreens again and Lisa cut in front of everyone in line.

"Sorry, everyone. She's mentally ill." Zach was so frustrated and looked apologetically at the other customers.

"You have no compassion for the mentally ill!" she yelled as she entered Ore-Ida's pin number. They drove home, where Lisa sat on the couch as her legs were starting to tingle.

Paging Dr. Baxter

Lisa knew she was off. She absolutely knew she just wasn't herself. She rapped out loud several times. "Paging Baxter…Paging Dr. Baxter! Paging Baxter… Paging Dr. Baxter. I need a pill, something Dr. Baxter!" She was so frustrated, and her legs were starting to tingle. She was scared that maybe she was going to have a heart attack, so she had Zach drive her to Kifer Hospital Urgent Care. They drove all over and could not locate urgent care.

She said, "Fuck it! Let's go to the ER!" After checking in, they took her vital signs, and everything checked out. "You mean I don't have to go to the hospital?" They said she was fine but they still had to run some blood tests and she wanted to jump for joy. Instead, she got up in front of the patients in the ER lobby and pumped her fist in the air. "I AM MENTALLY ILL! I AM MENTALLY ILL!" she shouted. She saw a lady wincing in pain in her wheelchair; Lisa told her it was going to be OK. She felt she could save everybody who was hurting.

"Sit down and behave," Zach said, looking annoyed, and she complied. She sat until they called her into an ER room. She lay in the bed for a few hours as they ran tests. She was cleared to go home. She was exhausted. She wanted to rest but her mind was racing.

Loved Ones and Healing

Lisa lay in bed talking to her friend Tully and told her she was tired. Tully told her to close her eyes while she sang her to sleep. Lisa must have slept for only about three hours. She wanted so badly to go back to sleep. Just the night before, she had been talking to Rina as her anxiety ran high. Rina comforted her at the time, but she still couldn't sleep.

Finally she was able to see Dr. Baxter on video chat, and he told her to increase the new medication dose and to use a sleep aid as well to get some rest. She and Zach were relieved after the appointment. Zach told Dr. Baxter that Lisa was ready to perform songs for him in frustration. Dr. Baxter laughed but was also very concerned for Lisa. After several days of taking the higher dose, Lisa started to come around and get back to the way she was normally. Although she sort of missed the high she felt in the mania, she was glad to be back to normal.

* * *

Alegra Saavepandria was Lisa's old high school friend. She was hilarious and made her laugh constantly. They were talking on the phone as Lisa was coming down from her mania. She needed friends to comfort her on the phone. She sat and talked to Alegra as she watched George Lopez on TV. She used laughter as a coping mechanism.

"So how are you, my dear?" Alegra asked. "What's going on?"

Lisa said, "I'm coming down from a manic episode, and George Lopez is really helping me."

"What? George Lopez? Are you like having dinner with him? Does he have a cousin?"

Lisa laughed. "No. I'm watching George Lopez on TV. He makes me laugh."

Alegra was disappointed but happy her dear friend was getting better.

* * *

Lisa would buy cigarettes, energy drinks, and beer for Zachariah almost every day. She saw Chaz from Extra Mile a lot to purchase these vices.

Chaz teased her as she asked for the cigarettes. "No! You can't have these!" And gave her a pleasant but teasing smile. He was a big, husky guy with facial hair. He had been very handsome as a young man. He was nice to look at, though, and his smile cheered Lisa up every time she saw him.

"You know these things aren't for me," she said, looking at all the vices on the counter.

Chaz said, "I know. I know you don't smoke and drink." He looked at her like he knew that it was obvious that they were for her husband. She was surprised that he'd figured that out. Lisa always looked for Chaz every time she walked into the store. One time she was hypomanic while Joey and Justin were in the van. She'd talked to Chaz for like twenty minutes until Joey came in to check on her. She'd been on the verge of a full-blown manic episode. Chaz probably knew she was a bit off, so he felt he needed to comfort her by telling her about his life little by little—his love interests, kids, ex-wife, and his previous jobs. Chaz was a godsend because Lisa found comfort in his smile and tender ways. He talked to her like she was somebody important.

* * *

Lisa knew Lana from high school choir. She was a dear friend, and they'd reconnected on social media. They talked on the phone, and Lana told Lisa she was an empath. Lisa wasn't sure what she meant at first, but Lana said it was like she could feel other people's emotions—she had empathy and love for all people. Lisa understood what she meant, and then they talked about their dark pasts and how they'd not been treated well by certain men in their lives. Lisa felt a connection with Lana and knew she could confide in her. She knew that even though she was manic, she could talk to Lana, and Lana would not judge her.

※ ※ ※

Lemasani was powerful. She was the strongest volleyball player Lisa had known in high school. They were tight and Lisa could confide in Lemasani. She found her on social media many years later and told Lemasani about her bipolar disorder, and Lemasani had nothing but love for her.

"Lisa, you were the one that encouraged me to play on the volleyball team. If it wasn't for you, I would have never played. I am so grateful for you."

Lisa felt so good to know she'd made a difference in Lemasani's life. Lemasani had grown children now, and Lisa was grateful for her, for social media, and for reconnecting with her dear friend, who had always been supportive of Lisa.

* * *

Lisa's dear friend Luisa was her ally. Luisa's son was Joey's friend since the second grade. They were in high school band together. Lisa and Luisa had a coffee date scheduled, but Lisa was feeling very manic; she had to cancel with Luisa.

She texted her, "Hi beautiful. I have to cancel our coffee date as I'm not feeling well. Estoy loca pero no loca." Lisa was trying to say "I'm crazy but not really crazy."

Luisa responded, "No you are not crazy, beautiful. We will see each other when you are feeling better."

Luisa was such a beautiful woman. She worked out and took good care of herself. She always kissed Lisa's cheek when she saw her and said, "Hello, beautiful!" She was beautiful on the inside as well as the outside. She supported Lisa with everything. She knew Lisa had a condition and many times offered her baked goods and tamales. She was so giving and loving to Lisa. Lisa turned to her dear friends for support even when she felt manic.

* * *

Lisa and Lina worked out together during their grad-school days. During grad school, when baby Zoey was three months old, Lisa told Lina that she had a manic episode and that she was recovering. They met for lunch, and Lina told Lisa that her best friend also had bipolar disorder, so she was familiar with it. Lina was her dear friend, and they sometimes connected on social media now that they lived far away from each other. Lina was a mother to three beautiful boys, and she loved Lisa dearly.

Mania and Performance

Lisa used to think of herself as a performer. She would act in her theater classes in college and sing in front of the congregation at church, sometimes about a hundred people. She would feel a burst of energy, a mini mania or hypomania, feeling so high on adrenaline. She would appear to be normal in her performances and everything would go well; it was the afterward part that was so manic.

After any performance she would harp on about the whole performance that night. She would think of every little note she sang, every little mistake she made in the lyrics or the lines of a monologue. She felt euphoric and did not sleep no matter how hard she tried. Her thoughts raced and her body felt so restless. Even though she lost sleep after performing, she still got out of bed the next morning as if she had slept for a few hours, and still felt energetic. Finally after a couple of days of mini mania, her body would crash and fall asleep, and she would sleep for most of the day. Lisa thought that mania was a good thing for her performance, a hypomania, though, a less severe mania. That nervous energy was what got her through her performances.

If she created a performance to reenact her manic episodes, she believed her mania would kick in. It might even kick in to the point of her needing to go to the hospital. Perhaps someday, when she felt comfortable with her whole self and felt the bipolar wouldn't get in the way of her performance, she would perform a reenactment. She wanted to share with many people out there what goes on during mania. Everyone was different and experienced various symptoms, some scarier than others. Lisa was an ordinary person with a story she wanted to share with the world; a performance just might be a good way to do it.

Lisa sat with her dad and sister Athena from another mother, one evening, talking to them about her bipolar disorder and how it really had affected her life. She told them that she laughed alone in her manias and that she also cried alone during her horrific depression. She hoped they could see her perform someday. Perhaps she could show everyone what it was like to have bipolar disorder, what it was like to have a mental illness.

Author's Final Thoughts

I hope I helped you in some way. Know that anyone can have bipolar disorder and can still be a human being. I want to tell Lisa's story to those that are going through the same thing. I want to help people. All I know is that if you know someone who is coping with a mental illness, be there for them. Lift them up when you can. Don't let them laugh and cry alone.

Author's Many Thanks

I would like to thank my mother, who always said I should write a book. Without my mom's encouragement, I would be lost. I would also like to thank my stepfather.

I thank my father for always being supportive of me and just being proud of me altogether. I thank my stepmother and my mother-in-law as well.

My partner's father in heaven is dear to my heart, and I thought of him while writing this book.

I thank all my beautiful sisters.

I thank my sister for designing the cover of this book.

I thank my brother-in-law and sister-in-law for also believing in me. I thank all my grandparents, both on earth and in heaven, and my aunts, uncles, nephews, and nieces for loving me unconditionally.

I thank all my cousins, who root for me each day. My cousin Scott P. is my guardian angel.

I thank my lifelong partner; he took care of me throughout everything. Without him, I would've been so lost. I thank my children for just being my world.

I thank many of my friends who were there for me: Brisha Y., Leilani N., Alejandra S., Maggie J., Vy T., Alie W., Daian O., Irene T., Dana M-P., Nita E., Tina L., Karen W., Zaki H., Anne Marie T., Issa C., Tempy R., Delores R., Janell P., Deanna F., Jay B., Dr. Byrd, Dr. Lee, Dr. Wander, Vivian B., Rita G., Tasha D., Jason F., Corrin C., Juan H., Kristina C., Russell H., and Erin H., Adrienne H., Deahna H., Sharon H., Gursharan K., Regina C., and Anessa M. You are all dear to my heart. Now, I will be working on my second book *Laughing and Crying Alone II*.

www.ingramcontent.com/pod-product-compliance
Lightning Source LLC
LaVergne TN
LVHW012023060526
838201LV00061B/4431